THE GEOGRAPHY OF LOGRAIRE

THE GEOGRAPHY OF LOGRAIRE

THOMAS MERTON

A NEW DIRECTIONS BOOK

Library of Congress Catalog Card Number: 78-88727
ISBN: 0-8112-0098-1

ACKNOWLEDGMENTS
The Trustees of The Merton Legacy Trust and the Publisher
express their gratitude to the authors, publishers and copyright
owners of the books, thus far identified and those still to be
identified, from which Thomas Merton quoted or paraphrased
in writing this book. More detailed acknowledgments will be
found in the Source Notes at the back of the book. Parts of
The Geography of Lograire were first published in the maga-
zines *Cimarron Review, Don Quixote, Gnomon, Green River
Review, Monk's Pond, The Outsider* and *Poetry*.

New Directions Books are published for James Laughlin
by New Directions Publishing Corporation,
333 Sixth Avenue, New York, 10014.

Manufactured in the United States of America.

Published simultaneously in Canada by McClelland and
Stewart, Ltd.

SECOND PRINTING

CONTENTS

EAST

WEST

AUTHOR'S NOTE

This is a purely tentative first draft of a longer work in progress, in which there are, necessarily, many gaps. This is only a beginning of patterns, the first opening up of the dream. A poet spends his life in repeated projects, over and over again attempting to build or to dream the world in which he lives. But more and more he realizes that this world is at once his and everybody's. It cannot be purely private, any more than it can be purely public. It cannot be fully communicated. It grows out of a common participation which is nevertheless recorded in authentically personal images.

In this wide-angle mosaic of poems and dreams I have without scruple mixed what is my own experience with what is almost everybody else's. Thus "Cargo" and "Ghost Dance," for instance, cease to be bizarre anomalies and are experienced as yours and mine as well as "theirs." But for this to be true, what is given of "Cargo" and "Ghost Dance" is most often literal and accurate quotation with slight editing and with of course much personal arrangement. And where more drastic editing is called for by my own dream, well, I have dreamed it.

Much also has been found in the common areas of nightmare to which we are all vulnerable (advertising, news, etc.). The most personally subjective part is perhaps the long meditation on Eros and Thanatos, centering in the New York City Borough of Queens, in the "North" canto.

I

But this dream also reaches out to London and other places in Europe. The focal point is around the gasometers of Elmhurst, the freight yards of Woodside, the crematory in Brooklyn, a Harlem nightclub, the boats in Bayside Bay, the tunnel under the East River leading into Manhattan. This meditation is surrealistic. "Top funnel house" is simply a sort of Hieronymus Bosch building which smokes and looks and is symbolic of death as a presence structured into society itself as guilt, police and undertakers. It is both police station, hospital and crematory which has devoured one by one the bodies of parents, grandparents, etc. Then there is the theme of Famous John as a sort of cloacal Mafia Id. And so on. The "South" canto is more self-evident. "East" and "West," "Cargo" and "Ghost Dance," play out in more universal and primitive myth-dream terms the same struggle of love and death, they enact the common participation of the living and the dead in the work of constructing a world and a viable culture. These poems incidentally are never explicitly theological or even metaphysical. The tactic is on the whole that of an urbane structuralism.

June, 1968

THE GEOGRAPHY OF LOGRAIRE

PROLOGUE: THE ENDLESS INSCRIPTION

1. Long note one wood thrush hear him low in waste pine
   places
   Slow doors all ways of ables open late
   Tarhead unshaven the captain signals
   Should they wait?

2. Down wind and down rain and down mist
   the passenger.

3. In holy ways there is never so much must

4. Should Wales dark Wales slow ways sea coal tar
   Green tar sea stronghold is Wales my grand
   Dark my Wales land father it was green
   With all harps played over and bells
   Should Wales slow Wales dark maps home
   Come go green slow dark maps green late home
   Should long beach death night ever come
   And welcome to dark father-mother land
   Simple white wall house square rock hill
   Green there low water hill rock square
   White home in dark bituminous con-
   Crete ways to plain of fates ways
   Fathers hill and green maps memory plain
   In holy green Wales there is never staying

5. Plain plan is Anglia so must angel father mother Wales
   Battle grand opposites in my blood fight hills
   Plains marshes mountains and fight
   Two seas in my self Irish and German
   Celt blood washes in twin seagreen people
   German Tristram is all mates' Grammer
   I had a toy called Tristram and Gurton's
   Needle in another sensitive place
   What Channel bard's boarder house next sweet
   Pub smell on cliff of winds Cliff was
   A welshest player on the rugged green at Clare
   Away next New Wood Forest fool on hunter map
   Ship of forests masts Spain masts in Beaulieu wood
   Minster in the New Wood Minster Frater in the grassy
   Summer sun I lie me down in woods amid the
   Stone borders of bards.

6. In holy walks there is never an order
   Never burden

7. Lay down last burden in green Wales seas end firs
      larches
   Wales all my Wales a ship of green fires
   A wall wails wide beside some other sex
   Gone old stone home on Brecon hill or Tenby harbor
   Where was Grandmother with Welsh Birds
   My family ancestor the Lieutenant in the hated navy
   From the square deck cursed
   Pale eyed Albion without stop.

8. In holy seas there is never so much religion.

9. On a run late hold one won
   Tarhead slaver captain selling the sables
   To Cain and Abel by design

4

10. Desire desire O sign of ire
    O Ira Dei
    Wrath late will run a rush under the
    Funnel come snow or deadly sign
    Design of ire rather I'd dare it not dare
    It not the ire run late hold strong Wales to a mast
    Young siren sexes of the green sea wash
    Hold captain home to Ithaca in a pattern of getaway
    Hold passion portion siren swinging porter
    Gutt bundle and funk gone
    Down slow mission done as possible
    And another child of Wales
    Is born of sea's Celts
    Won rock weeds dragon designs
    Missions capable defenders

11. In frail pines should they sometimes wait
    Or ponds said one space cotton in captain design
    Trace a dark pine fret way work walks
    In soft South Pine house eroded away
    Sweet smelling Virginia night and mint
    Should they wet those cotton patches
    Wash out a whole town

12. Wash ocean crim cram crimson sea's
    Son Jim's son standing on the frigate
    Jim Son Crow's ocean crosses a span
    Dare heart die Spanish ram or Lamb Son's Blood
    Crimson's well for oceans carnate sin sign
    Ira water Ira will not wash in blood
    Dear slain son lies only capable
    Pain and Abel lay down red designs
    Civil is slain brother sacred wall wood pine

Sacred black brother is beaten to the wall
The other gone down star's spaces home way plain

13. Dahomey pine tar small wood bench bucket
    Under shadow there wait snake
    There coil ire design father of Africa pattern
    Lies all eyes awake eroded night
    Traces gone tire far traces of dawn's fire
    Dead rope hang cotton over captain branch

14. The willing night hides everything
    Wills it tar face fret work wash out all chain
    Saving all one country slave
    Snake and tarheel minister and bat
    And blood and ram and Isaac done in a dare.

15. Plain Savior crosses heaven on a pipe

16. Hay Abraham fennel and grass rain ram under span's
    star
    Red grow the razors in the Spanish hollow

17. Hallow my Savior the workless sparrow
    Closes my old gate on dead tar's ira slam
    Gone far summer too far fret work blood
    Work blood and tire tar under light wood
    Night way plain home to wear death down hard
    Ire hard down on anger heel grind home down
    Wary is smashed cotton-head beaten down mouth
    When will they all go where those white Cains are dead?

18. Sign Redeemer's "R"
    Buys Mars his last war.

SOUTH

I

Will a narrow lane
Save Cain?

The Lamb the killer's friend
Skinned in meetings
Has a raw road and it may rain

WE ALL KNOW CAIN MAY BE THE LONGER RUNNER

High stocks buy Betterman's
Sweet Rosy Country Cross
Captain's a wanted Rosicrucian
Traitor to peevish liquor
Kills a brother in the outside lane

LAMB ADMITS TIES TO CAIN

Flashlight umbrella
Casts blood beam
On Daisy Violet Zinnia
Buttercup Rose
Angry under some steps,
Some rain!

Cain and Daisy lock their golden eyes
We all know Cain
But can a Lamb save Cain the raider?

"Maybe he has two manors one for Sundays
One for weeks anger kicked out nigger
Don't come no more white nigger door
Keep out of here"

Go back sore to wait writing
Where happiness beasts will wait behind a store
A bloody sight for sore eyes
"Top fun for D Tremens above the waist"

HOW WOULD YOU LIKE TO LIVE IN THIS PLACE?

It may be two men met Sunday ten
Wearing their whole wheat hats
Saw Satan with a dark knife cut tobacco
When High Green and Corngod stand together
Over Kentucky's corrugated temper
All wet nightlife to Cain and waif

TEN GUNS ARE OUT OF WORK UP ANGER HOLLOW

Try outsmart Saturday's night air
Tight teller sees city split where
Manmade bloodrains light and chemistry wet
Upon blue grass signs the red flower forever

AND KEEP CAIN OUT OF THAT HOLLOW

"I think we owe you an apology mister part time revolver
Mister tallhat individual smell
All sixfoot fires began on Mars landing Friday
When they found the oilwell"

Light police phone spark starter ten a dollar
All fire marcher explodes an invention
Gates are out a million
Try outstart capricious air
Mister tallhat revolver is everywhere

WHY WILL NOT LAMBS STAY FOREVER WELL IN SKINS?

It may be two men met Sunday ten with a happiness beast
A raw Lamb coming from the hollow
Tied to killer Bishops for the feast

100,000 Negroes most of whom have thin black skin
Tinderfoot passover dry edge light wells away
Blowup a million

TEMPER IS CANDY TO CAIN'S DAISY

In meetings red with Rosy pies
All were had by a good time up Ash's hollow

One narrow lane saved Lamb's friend Paschal Cain

II

1. Roar of red wood racer eats field. Green breakaway go cars light lanes. A robber lends the money. Aluminum gates grand open. Riverchange alongside lights. Mist downstairs. Riverhouse brown: green the riverrace. Mist down stairs. Mist lights. The getaway!

2. Must armyboys craterbodies blown down today tankway? Spill river. Mist. Giant bridge finds way to woman. Silence mimes rivercity. Gate to wettest summers in the South.

3. Roar of red wood rover lights army. Way station all the road to end of one more day. My day. The wandering oculist takes his homework train. Sad red hillside of houses search night. Police begin their shine.

4. Smokeshot low Fort Thomas. Nineteenth century mothers hazel in hell. Push sandy button strike the phone. Soft brazen Sunday hello SUN! It is a sunny day at last through the Hudepohl mist. I am the lonely one whose name is scratched on the plate. I am the lonely photo above giant water. I am the way to Louisville in the end. Doorway sun and the fern. If I went. I am the lonely grey police boat also.

5. I am the crane in stark south flight.

6. Red lover stations all along that road. Riverchance along mist buildings. Silverchange under steel span. Here sun! Here soft smoke siren. Gold plant swings destroyer riverlights up and down. Here examine smoke far down river. Study woman question afraid. Here. Examine the Churches. Wait station. Wait Covington station. Way north. The hazel points of her two visions. Hazel had nine mothers in the same city. Crane has money. Crane opens the aluminum gates. Enters winner.

7. Examine onion Church. Best old copper green spire in German sun. Gone Churches priest examines money book confess detail. Army is here. Churches are here. Gambles omens. Gone Germans. Gone Hudepohl Beer. Here. Sidelights. Riverdays. Wide riverdays. Wide summers. Shock of armies. Lights. Police. All hope destroyed forever. Police aim long light feel bridge. Lightfinger wants detail. Lightfinger love's trigger. Races change.

8. Wet street. Change. Ring Cincinnati. Wake daycolor. Neosubstance comes to life in hospital. She makes wide frightwindows. Haze. Southward goes the sun.

9. Make change. Race electric air. Phone the home. Make every daycolor square indoors very tired. Secure waiting away. Wasting money says hello. Deodorant here today. Stands daycolor change at white desk so sweet. Smell the blonde blushes O. Aim for the lonely waist says Gringo.

10. Green breakaway go all cars light suns. Breakaway change wet stars riverlanes. Night south riverlanes home. Signs spell St. Louis. High power must wire here connect all space. Crosstrack rages seven states. Light runs south

and hello smiles Alabama hello smiles hello. Waiting anyhow says Army Sam. Army waits in vain.

11.   Seven states. Now floodlight occupies neo-fleuve. Neon bitch smiles at police racket. High fire spends all night fun. Wasting away without a tremble. Wasting phones hello say seven states. Hello power boats alert river. Traffic never dreamt so wide. Change. Run for the lonely night says Gringo. But we are never alone.

12.   Boats alert. City all awake. Carrolton, Louisville, Owensboro, Paducah. Gates open for Victors. Light is neo-strange. Music of lighted copperheads all over town. Wake daycolor neo-sand-storm-stars down city. Orange is awake.

13.   Neo-wristwatch kills whitey dead. He was just unlucky.

14.   High speed ends connect space. Now speak. Say Fort Knox is home of armor.

15.   Maxwell you son of a bitch get off my place.

16.   We all made it to the track on a dirty bet. Sorrow has a wet face. A sign: "All losers leave by west gate."

17.   Hazel wins. Fresh is the sandwich.

18.   Through Knox at nightfall. Armycrater boys face down on the wet table. The grey mistrivers of night. Nightfall lights up houses. Redgrain music beat down houseflats. A ghost dancer walks in a black hat through gates of horn.

III. HYMNS OF LOGRAIRE

1. Nearer my God to rock of eyes
   Or to my chariot of thee
   That is Elias rider of red skies

   Nearer my cherubim
   To the crimson fruit
   In chariot three

   Wishing everybody well
   From now to Monday.

2. Sign on the dome:
   "Expect thy next tread
   Don't tread on the marine."

3. You were sixteen
   My village queen
   Shining in sunpeel paint
   With your strip all recent
   From customary behavior

   You stood alarmed
   O darkeyed think
   Full to the very barrels
   And I wished you cunning
   Glasses and all

Which was the time
We broke the furniture
Trying to get me over
My own wall.

IV. MIAMI YOU ARE ABOUT TO BE SURPRISED

You are going to be pleasantly surprised by this
You will find yourself sweetly insulted
By earphones and you will also
Be pleasantly wet
Where you are going

For you shall make expensive waves
Meeting the answer to women's questions
In a swift novel of suspense

IF YOU HAVE HEART FAILURE WHILE READING THIS
THE POET IS NOT RESPONSIBLE

And you will meet a lot of friends
Falling into hopeless spray
As if that were what you wanted
And limbo dancing (non-lethal)
Will focus the muscles of science
On your waistline
You can't control so many
Wonderful people

When you become exotic bait
For a suburban afternoon
Well you wanted to stay in focus
But did you?

ALL NIGHT LONG WHEN YOU CAN'T STAND IT HERE
TAKE IT OR CRACK
WHERE ELSE CAN YOU FIND IT
IN A CAN?

You are going to be warned
By a gourmet with a mouthful of seaweed
Reaching all the way through superb
Armholes

He will try to help you decode
Your own scrambled message
Teach you your own way
As if you wanted that
Will you please try?

And you will be surprised
By Hilton candlelight
With more than the usual bill
(Unless you are pregnant)

Our new method takes you out of the stream
Of cold function
But you have to bend
Like all our other gamebirds
While you are gently made over
All the way down to the jawline
You don't have to be young in years
For the machine to register your secret desires
Which are never secret and always foolish

So you are about to be surprised.

V. TWO MORALITIES

THONGA LAMENT (Africa)

Look the blue oxen
Come down from the altars
To your caverns O Fathers
I stay outside your tunnels
Do you see them coming
The oxen
O Fathers?
Blue oxen into the caverns.
You gave me life O Father
But now you are gone
Now you are secret
Living in famous tunnels
(But where?)
Let us eat together in peace
Let us not disagree
That I and my children
May live long here outside
Out here in the air
Without coughing or swaying
Or losing balance and falling
Into the tunnels
Look O Father
The blue oxen are coming
They will find you
In the caverns.

HARE'S MESSAGE (Hottentot)

One day Moongod wanted to send a message to man. Hare volunteered to go to man as Moongod's messenger. "Go tell men," said Moon, "that they shall all rise again the way I also rise after each dying." But Hare the messenger deceived man, changing the heavenly message to one of earth. "You must die," he said, "just as I do." Then Moon cursed Hare. And the Nagama must now never eat Hare's meat. They do not eat Hare the runner for the runner is death.

VI. A CLEVER STRATAGEM:
OR, HOW TO HANDLE MYSTICS

When I was out in the Nyasaland Missions we held a meeting of five thousand converts at which religious fervor naturally mounted to the highest pitch. So much intensity of religious feeling required to be carefully channeled to prevent outbursts. Fervor must not be permitted to dissipate itself in wasteful, even riotous disorders. One morning two of the leading teachers came to report some experiences they were having. They had been out in the bush all night praying and they had felt their bodies lifted up from the earth while bright angelic beings came to meet them as they ascended. What did this mean? I replied not in word but in deed. I went to the dispensary, took down the salts, gave them each a stiff dose and sent them off to bed. The visions and ascensions immediately ceased, and were replaced by a sweetly reasonable piety that disturbed no one. A missionary must combine spiritual passion with sound sense. He must keep an eye on his followers.

VII. NOTES FOR A NEW LITURGY

There's a big Zulu runs the congregation
A woe doctor cherubim chaser
Puts his finger on the chief witch
Has a mind to deter foes
Is by the Star Archangel shown a surprise
Writes his letters in vision mentions his B.A.
From many a college
Has a fan to scatter flies
Receives a penetrating look
From an imaginary visitant in white
Knows all the meanings at once
Knows he is in heaven in rectangles
Of invented saints
Flaming with new degrees and orders every day

"I dreamt this Church I dreamt
Seven precious mitres over my head
My word is final.

"I now General Overseer Concession Registrar
Of Rains and Weather Committeeman
For Pepsi-Cola all over the veldt
Flail of incontinent clergy
Wave my highstrung certificate in times of change
Don't you need a Defender with a medical guarantee?

"You think that I am only a clown-healer from
    the out-district?

Hold this black bag while I lay hands on children
Steady my followers with magic curios
When I sleep I watch you with eyes in my feet
Last night I dreamt of four beds
I must marry again must go get
Another angel-nun
Come holy deaconess we'll ride
Barefoot in yellow busses to Jordan River
Wearing emblems of the common vow

"Subleaders keep telling the message
Like it was new
Confirming my charism as Prime-Mover in Management
I shall continue in office as President
For all time until the earth melt
As all Full-Leaders stand over you wearing their watches
Moulding you by government of thought
And I return a while to the Origin
Ruling through a female medium from an obscure place:

"HOLD THIS MITRE WHILE I STRANGLE CHICKENS
AND THROW THEM IN THE AIR
COVERING THE SACRED STONE WITH BLOODY FEATHERS
(And surround the altar
With lie detectors.)"

VIII.   CE XOCHITL: THE SIGN OF FLOWERS
(Mexico)

Men born under Ce Xochitl are cheerful and ingenuous
Inclined to music and pleasure, witty talkers.
The women hard workers and free with their bodies.

(Sahagun)

1. Xochipilli, the Flower Giver:
   They fast in his honor.
   His movable feast: Xochilhuitl.

2. If any man had access to a woman
   Or woman to man in those four fast days
   They spoiled their offering
   Offended the Flower God who would punish
   Their secret parts with boils, buboes,
   Chancres and other rottings.

3. Some ate no chili others at midnight
   Took their corn soup with a flower
   Floating in the middle.
   They call this the "Fast of Flowers."

4. Month nine: in fields and patches
   Of corn gather flowers
   Bring them in armfuls
   To the feasting house
   Keep them overnight
   Then at dawn

Make thick garlands
For the god's yard and day.

5. That same eve the people
   Killed hens and little dogs
   Plucked hens singed dogs
   Made tamales
   Up all night
   Getting ready

6. Danced on the god's day
   Warriors and boys
   And public women
   Snaking and singing
   With no sidestep no turns
   No gestures but slow
   Solemn composed
   In perfect time
   Led by those expert in war
   With arms around the waists
   Of their partners
   As though embracing
   (Which the other dancers
   Were not allowed to do)

7. *Yax Coc Ah Mut*
   Feast of the Green Turtle
   They dance on tall stilts
   Offering the god corn liquor
   Peacocks' heads

   Dancers come with little clay dogs
   And bread.

A dog with black shoulders that is virgin
Is sacrificed.

"Such were the services which their demons commanded
them."

(Bishop Landa)

IX. THE LADIES OF TLATILCO

1. Effigy vessels shapes of apes
   Men peccaries rabbits coons ducks acrobats and fish
   Long charming little bottlenecks pots bowls
   And inventions:
        For example
   "when liquid was poured out of the funnel-shaped tail
   the animal's ears whistled softly
   in a double gurgling note."

                       (Covarrubias)

2. Mixtec urn: Old man tiger crown holds dog nine.

3. Nine deer effigy coonsong
   Fondest little bowl
   Offered to songstruck dead
   Maize and cactus milk
   Small red beer
   Peppers and chilis in bowls
   Of warm red clay.

   Living acrobats stand in a pyramid.

4. "If they carved wood we shall never know it."

5. Look his brute spear nails placename
   Look he has a glyph
   Stone eye sees conqueror date
   (Too late).

6. The ladies of Tlatilco
   Wore nothing but turbans
   (Skirts only for a dance)
   A lock of hair over the eyes
   Held only by a garland
   Tassels and leaves
   They bleached their black hair
   With lime
   Like the Melanesians.

7. Feminine figurines with two heads or with four eyes
       and ears
   Two noses or doublemouth on the same head
   "Reminiscent of Picasso
   Perhaps connected with idea of twins."

8. A most provocative perfume
   Wicked wicked charms
   Natural spray dispenser
   A special extract
   For four-eyed ladies of fashion
   MY SIN
   "And my most wicked provocative lewd
       dusting-powder excitements."
   (Two noses on the same head)

9. The most thoughtful gift of the year
   With a Queen Anne Rose (Patent No. 3,187,782)
   Budding with terry-loops
   (Two nuns fighting for the same towel)

10. A flowering bath
    Your long-stem skin

Your patent rose
Is all in loops
Is all in tones
Bleach your black hair
With a coat of lime
And dance in your turban.

11. I saw two moons
In dreadful sweat
"Fit perfectly under
A rounded collar jacket"
I saw two moons
In shades of toast
Coming to calm my fright
Sweet Mother Rose
Ann Gypsy Nun
In a new trim
Toast collar.
I saw two moons
Coming from a certain kind of store
Where the ladies of Tlatilco
Wear nothing but sweaters
Bleach their black hair with lime
Or look like fire clay
Reddening their hair with dye
From seeds of achiote.

12. Two ways to tell a primitive bath figurine.
With an expensive book
Your skin can tell
"All her goings graces"
In taupe or navy
Cashmere lovat wine

In maize my moons
O so serene
In cardigan charcoal blue
Shetlands hunter green

Two ways to tell a primitive
Nun fighting for
A towel.

13. O patent Gypsy London Rose
     On fire with inventions
     Looking out of a red hood
     Upon acrobats shaved heads
     Wizards and trumpeters

14. O fervent Gypsy Blue we love your diamonds
     We are Boston experts and we understand
     "the whole actively involved female world"
     Which is red
     With achiote seeds
     Rich in naseberries octaniques
     Otaheite apples
     Having great fun in a natural spray
     Dispenser of SIN
     With lime like the Melanesians

     But Picasso
     Was *not* thinking of twins!

X. CHILAM BALAM (Yucatan)

1. "They came to Tísip
   With pepper in their speech
   In 11 Ahau
   Cleared cornfields
   Built a city."

2. They were received like Fathers
   With nodding plumes at the well's edge
   In Itza
   Thus they were called the "Itzaes."

3. Sunrise. New Kingdom.
   Fresh wakes sweet tropic earth!
   Tribute paid in cotton
   For the Four Men
   (North South East West)
   In Chichen.

   Then the Lords
   Rich in cotton
   Meet Gods
   Equal in voice to Gods
   And those whose voices
   Were not equal to Gods' voices
   Were thrown into the well
   To cry louder.

4. Then came Laws
   High pyramids
   Thirteen Itzaes in majesty
   With pepper in their prayers
   Made deals with the Raingods
   In clouds of smoke.

5. "Our Gods have grown bigger" they said
   Then bitter times began
   The plain smoked
   All the way to the sea.

6. Thirteen katuns they ruled.
   Until the treason of Hunac Ceel
   Driven from their cities into jungle
   4 Ahau was the katun
   The wail of lives
   Thirteen katuns of suffering and law
   And they were called in the end
   "The Remnant of Itzaes"
   The last few built Mayapan
   "Maya men"
   Was their new name.

7. Lamentation
   Priests of Xiu
   Slow along the cavern wall
   From altar to altar
   On the well's rim.

8. "The priest asks for green bark. Thirteen times he
   strips all flowers and all leaves off the branches. He
   strips them utterly bare. He binds the stripped branches
   in a bundle. Katuns without hope!"

9. Prayer in the cavern
   For the last time
   Pitch dark well
   Stopping at the altars
   Blind fingers explore the faces
   Of rock signs
   Figures cut in the wall
   Spell: "Justice exists"
   "Heaven exists"
   And the prophet Chilam answers
   Hix binac hix mac
   (Maybe yes maybe no)
   "But now we carry the sons of Itza on our backs like boulders."
   And the priests have come to the end of submission. The end of desire.
   They are about to destroy themselves because of the injuries done to our people.

10. FACE OF THE PRIEST CHILAM WHEN HE IS ON THE POINT OF ENTERING THE WELL OF THE CAVERN.

XI. DZULES (Yucatan)

1. "EVERY MOON EVERY YEAR EVERY WIND MUST TRAVEL AND
   PASS ON
   EVERY BLOOD ALSO COMES AT LAST TO ITS PLACE OF REST
   JUST AS IT COMES BRIEFLY TO ITS POWER AND THRONE."

   (*Chilam Balam*)

2. 11 Ahau signals the landing
   Dzules from the east
   Terror out of the sea
   Withering the flowers

3. "TO MAKE THEIR OWN FLOWER OPEN THEY SACKED AND
   SMASHED THE FLOWER OF OTHERS"

4. 11 Ahau the rising of bearded men
   Who take away the white clothing
   Long gone are the days
   Of the honey-offering

5. They bring down all power smash man to earth make
   green skies
   Weep blood hard and heavy is the maize bread of this
   katun
   Strangled is the flute-hero the painter Yaxal Chuen
   the jeweler
   The Ape Ixkanyultu "Precious Voice"
   His throat is now cut gods driven out
   Singers scattered gone is Kay Nicté

34

The flower dance around the rock pool
Canta la mujer joven
To call back gone man made gentle as a
Tame animal with dance with charm
To the sweet body lying in the water
Covered with jungle flowers
Dispersados serán por el mundo las mujeres que cantan
Y los hombres que cantan
Y todos los que cantan.

6. AY ENTRISTEZCÁMONOS PORQUE LLEGARON!

7. "You shall feed them" (said the prophecy) "you shall wear their clothing you shall use their hats and you shall talk their language. But their sentences shall speak division."

8. AY ENTRISTEZCÁMONOS PORQUE LLEGARON!

9. "They are destroyed,
The omens."
Days and nights
Show the way
"Pay heed to the truth which I give you
In the katun of dishonor."

10. "During five days Ix Haunab, Mother Despair, Ix Huznab, Mother Terror, Ix Kuknab, Mother of Lies, eat from the red-painted bowl, from the white-painted bowl, from the black-painted bowl and from the yellow-painted bowl."

11. MUCHO Y COMPLETO ADULTERIO SERÁ LA OCCUPACIÓN DE TODOS!

12. With brimming tears
    We mourn our lost writings
    The burned books
    The burned men
    The flaming harvests
    Holy maize destroyed
    Teachings of heaven and earth
    Destroyed.

13. The wooden books
    Burned before our eyes
    At the well.

14. We pray the eyes of our sons
    May one day read again
    The stone writings.

15. Silly pigeons
    Pass as men
    Birds to be detested
    They shoot others
    Through the heart.
    Do hummingbirds cheat one another?
    Do they kill one another?

16. No one who travels a bad road
    Ever arrives. The people
    Weigh every word.
    Will lies
    Never end?

17. We have burned sweet copal
    On account of the hangings.

18. *Justitia* = vex Christians.

36

19. Four katuns
    We ate grass
    Don Antonio Martinez
    Guest of our Nobles
    "Xaul is his name
    As one who aspires to heaven"
    Little by little
    We are degraded
    Wives of our aristocrats
    Take money
    To sleep with enemies

20. "I shall yet prove my name:
    It is Martinez."

21. Do hummingbirds cheat one another?

22. LLEGARON LOS HOMBRES DE DIOS DEL ORIENTE LOS QUE
    TRAYERON EL DOLOR.

23. On a day of 9 Oc
    Arrival of the turkey cocks
    Strutting and gobbling
    Redneck captains with whips
    Fire in their fingers
    Worse than Itzaes
    Friars behind every rock every tree
    Doing business
    Bargaining for our souls
    Book burners and hangmen
    Sling the high rope
    They stretch the necks
    Lift the heads
    Of priest and noble
    Our calendar is lost

Days are forgotten
Words of Hunab Ku
Counterfeit
The world is once again
Controlled by devils
We count the pebbles of the years
In hiding:
Nothing but misfortune.

24. PROTECT THE LIVES OF YOUR POLICE PUT OUT THE SMALL
FIRES WITH FOG OR FOAM MARK THE TROUBLEMAKERS WITH
DYE MOVE THE CROWD WITH WATER-BASED IRRITANTS KEEP
THE CROWDS AWAY FROM THE CAR WITH ELECTRICITY DRIVE
THE SNIPERS OUT OF HIDING WITH TEAR GAS GRENADES
BREAK UP CROWDS WITH SMOKE

25. Memory of the katuns and years swallowed up by
the red moon!
"Then fire devoured the people of Israel and
the prophets."

(Chilam Balam)

A lively business in police helicopters.

26. "One hundred and fifty years later there was an agree-
ment with the foreigners. That is what you are paying
for. There was a war between the whites and the peo-
ple here, the men who used to be great captains of the
nation formerly. That is what you are paying for now."

27. The year fifteen hundred and forty one of the Dzules
1541—day 5 Ik 2 Chen.
*"A high-frequency blower that delivers a banshee howl
beyond the tolerance of human ears."*

NORTH

PROLOGUE

WHY I HAVE A WET FOOTPRINT ON TOP
OF MY MIND

To begin a walk
To make an air
Of knowing where to go
To print
Speechless pavements
With secrets in my
Forgotten feet
Or go as I feel
Understand some air
Alone
Around the formerly known
Places
Like going
When going is knowing
(Forgetting)

To have passed there
Walked without a word
To have felt
All my old grounds
Forgotten world
All along
Dream places
Words in my feet

41

Explain the air of all
Feel it under (me)
Stand
Stand in the unspoken
A cool street
An air of legs
An air of visions

Geography.
I am all (here)
There!

I. QUEENS TUNNEL

1. Top the burning funnel house with watchman's eyes.
Pointed otherside reckoning bridge. Courtside Queens paddy
wagon. Smoketop funnel house Addy Daddy Wagon. With
Sam's Tuna all lighted up. Very funny tunnels of Breughel
at Coney. Coney Queen's lights down into sudden tunnel.
Spinners. The quick brown bus. Lousdog hit that moon.
Gone. Lazy mummies stored in a locked room.
Rivers ever ways light dark down.
Top the burning light everlasting insurance all over this
downtown construction.
Woolforth budding up in the light. Look up to it from tun-
nels. Top the five and ten funnel smoking a little lightly
up.
Brookly river sing my orange song: rickety bridge to the
funeral parlor.
Life and death are even.
My Lady Mum is all alive in Homer. May might be in love
poems or others. Quick into another tunnel.
Van is in the apartments where he used to sing. His girl is
kept in a trunk. Food for novel. Baskets of flowers. My
Bunny lies over the station. At Queen's Plaza.
They come with baskets of bread. Italian bread. Mafia
Geography. Sicily in Queens.
Name one bisquit factory near Woodside. I can. Sunshine
before the tunnel.
Tracks all home by boxy meadow come. Manmountain
winner. Mafia alp. Name a stadium with a sign for cough
medicine. Castoria riverrun coughdrum. Put under a blan-
ket into his tunnel: the Italian champ. Won.

The funnel house moves looking all over the then wide country and down come planes full of Mafia fightfixers.

Tops of the apartments at pillbox hills firing tennis at Jews. Out of the roars come vendors. It am tutor at Kew to a tennis. Tennis Latin for the Long Island RR. Backandforth to drum drum bubber. Funnel top is watching you. The kettle moves away from the burners.

A BUILDING SPEAKS: "TURN LEFT FOR THE RACETRACK. THIS IS THE GEOGRAPHY OF LOGRAIRE."

2. Topsmart cunnels with memorial Chaplin. He went off pilgrim smart with the collection. Run run the clever captain all over Queens. Van is in the cunning apartment with his novel. A flight of pigeons with discipline. I sold my wagon. I lost my labels in the funny tunnel of scream.

3. Most holy incense burners of Elmhurst save us. Most Coronas screen us. House of Hungarians feed us. Give us our Schenley labels from day to day. Give us our public lessons of love. Swimming grunt lights down to the bottom. Even the Island is long won. Trams to the end. House of Hungarians spare us. Holy incense burners of Elmhurst dissolve us. Trains come and gone. Their own hot smell and passage snuffed entirely under. Save us. *Englouti!* Periodic swallowing of travel under the East Sound. Then Hellgate. Dread! Winterdazzle yards of the metropolitan asshole. Most holy incense burners. Smoking tops. Crowns of Mafia. Caruso with his boxtops all over the train. Corona. Then the dumps. Deserve us!

4. Spider track out: spike out some home.

Rattle away to legendary capitals of the Rulers of Lograire.

A land of sandpits here without a single mountain. There go lemons.
Every boy is called Francis.

5. Tracks all home by boxy meadow of champs. Caruso won the top part of the box. He won the whole house. I jeered in the night at fans. I fled from shadowfixers.

6. Lawrence was big and weak with glasses. I despised him at the station. The high sand wall nearby became the place of an apartment. There Lois lived all tiny in a box of candy. I kept her there in case I had a novel. I met her by the lamp. We swam together in ginger ale. The big detective he sat downstairs running the timetables and commanding trains. The dark son of the tugboats married his daughter. The detective told one train after another to circle through Lograire. Dalzell told the tugs and lighters to circle the harbor. Boyer was next door with pictures of his tugboats in the attic. I knew where all the boats came from. I knew all the topdecks of Olympic. Lois and I knew the top of the radio building where I watched. You could not hear ourselves smiling while we trailed together to Sylvania Station. You had to be young then to act foolish in dens. Top funnel house was watching with pointed eyes.

7. It was light week in Lograire and all the phones. Sleepy time under the thickest summers. Insect lights and swings. Mortal tinkle of porches and glasses. Rumrunners call up Edison "inviting you to Charleston." Some sleepy-time man is coming down the island with his saxophone. Uncle Sled laughs across the street on other porches. I am sleepy-time with insects as they hum. The humdrum screen. The lawnmower morning. The hot garden is my hideaway

from the whisperer. I think of clouds. I think alone under the maple.

8. It was light week in Lograire and all the phones. I am back from Curaçao she said. (They have wires in their voices when they want in Lograire.) When they want you should come by train to the tunnels. Breughel very funny under the city. When they want you should come via Elmhurst (save us the burners) via the gastank via the town. Queens burners defend tunnel.

Ruthie had a friend a big fink from Ohio too big for the apartment. He was too big for that bathroom. He blew down three walls.

Very fast cars in and out the poles under the Woodside elevated.

Name a factory where they make bathrooms: big ones, little ones. Bill worked for the bathrooms.

Head for the funnels into the city of verticals.

Stark hot stacks all night, stacklights, piles, Edisons, orders. The buildings rise full of orders up under lighted planes. Up. I remember. Back from Curaçao she told. Come and see why I have wires in my voice for you now. All of a sudden. I cannot come, I said. I have dead people to attend to. I have to travel the gastanks again to Elmhurst.

The grey-eyed Church is gonna get me I said.

Blue sides in the fishery shop I said, the wines and Mafias of Corona.

I have wires in my voice for you to come she said. I come in very fast cars if I can make it I replied if I can make it past Elmhurst.

9. It was light week in Lograire. The wine was free. Connie had a bowl. All the boys' names were Frank. He went

46

all the way to the drugstore to be sick on account of military school. Phones rang. Cops' cars came and went looking at the party.

Anna had a relative in a field and the field had a speakeasy. Connie had an inn called Connie's Inn. Music under the hot tunnels of summer. The cops were in the cellar wanting to do the Charleston with the German maid. Connie had on a wet bathrobe and Frank got sick in the maid's bathroom on account of military school. We went to sleep in a boat that night in the harbor singing in front of fat Tony's. The boats were all beyond the reach of Edison and played their own lights upon the harbor. Several called Frank went all the way. I knew they took him in a copscar from the middle of the Park. I knew Finneran would fall in the middle of Harlem. Some stayed in the boats and others went to Cambridge.

10. All the walls have high grey teeth and tickle the night with signs. All the nights are children of chicken movies. We came home early only to write back to the same movies: "wishing you were here!" The city of verticles. The verses of comicals. The time had come for Auld Lang Syne to forget and for the business to part companies.

11. Don't tromp on the Macaire. Tonton Macoute is in the area. Watch the manholes. Protect the lives of your police. Lively traffic on all the phones. Helicops.

12. Famous John is downstairs under the speakeasy. He is conducting all the spillways. He is the demiurge of all ways out: a devil of a toilet. If you don't know Macaire you can't make it to the subways. But Famous John is sinister: he runs the undertow of a big city. It is all controlled

from under Sugar Hill—the Hill where the diamonds are, where Finneran fell, the diamonds' eyes, Edison's elves, living and loving in nighty coves.

Famous John lives under all the nightspots in an invisible office. He is the city's liver.

If you know Macaire he can fix it for you to get away. But Ruthie has a friend. A big girl from Vassar College. Mum in a tent. Followed by graffiti.

13. Famous John puts a sign on the door: Tonight baby all the Edisons are going to blink.

A message from Sugar Hill: "Famous John is writing his name on your apartment door."

Try to call the Edisons and see if they are still in business. You can't do this anymore. You have to pay Macaire. Tonton sticks his funny head up out of the manholes. Yes, everywhere.

14. Famous John is inviting you to a wondrous trip with his spies. A ride in roofless vans to see tall smokes all over the experience: the smokes of Edison, the spinning winter bridges, the lovelorn whooping crane, the warehouses of Coney's unbeatable fun. Famous John is inviting you to drink at Connie's Inn where the bowl is for everybody. Winedark East River for everybody. And on the winegarbage waters of Spuyten Duyvil we race Big John the New York Central Steamer with our plucky college shell. Insane. Famous John is inviting you to the Catskills for a lightning summer. Observe poetry in a spell. Coney Island with trees and a waterfall.

15. Top the funnel house eyes roving everywhere to watch for Jews and Christians doing it. All the eyes of analysis:

48

you are counted as you pass through Astoria. All the eyes
of the planes coming down. Freightyards of Armageddon.
The whole city is full of passengers. It is a seeing city; a
singing telephone. Top of funnel house (won by Caruso)
is big know-how—counts police helicopters. All the eyes of
Jews and Christians are locked in a treasure computer. Top
the funnel house eyes tell exactly where you must go.
Every way you turn your car it is still there: the electric.

16.   Madmen in a vacant lot bet on a walking kettle.
A runner gets his foot caught in the teeth of a field. Cola
gardens around the clock intent golf counters win. Never
mind. The fight is over furniture, over a bowl, over a
lighter, over a burner. The city is observed by invisible
buzzards of silk. And a big fat ass from Ohio is a sitter in
Elmhurst. Top the funnel house eyes know wherever you
go, to the burners, to the houses, to the chapels, to the
stores. Who can win? When he raped Kitty in these streets
all the people turned away and pretended not to notice.

17.   The sacred books are confiscated by police to keep eyes
under sightless dome. Study famous text in court. Sacred
words kept shut in horny room. They keep my novels in a
box of candy. Shine continental glad warm being in Law.
Witness defies sentence structure. Chatterly wins sightless
connection in timeworn nickle viewer: hierarchic spectacle.
Eyes down everyone. Fold hands, walk aisles, composures,
make up for Lawrence in Church. Save famous continental
dome from Reds. Extort glad news from Receiver. Famous
John will live in hiding with "Roses of Life." Latest sacred
arrested books saved up in jealous Senates of memory for
more fun until better business. Keep eyes ahead gone dead
dome: a shiny bald Church with a hole in the head a

veritable pantheon. Fulltime overwork for Monsignori canonizing randy films. Keep sacred religious motions private. Italian cineasts watch Cardinal taking a bath. Sacred ideas confiscated twice by eminent machine. Good news dame is apprehended and shut up in extended thought. Business reverses blind control and gets better. Cardinal relents and warm room smells great. Author blesses Ruthie's fat friend. Forgiveness all round. Sacred books confined to ecclesiastical pen. Keep ageless roses in cardinal's warm bedroom. Wishing you the wonders of our episcopal garden. Lost his glasses reading books in secret buildings. Never found again. Pantheon doorman saves pleasure dome from detection.

18. See you home under the lamp of lights in guise of protection. Harlem.

19. Sendings: a powder. Stays. Pomade. Twill. Rawhide. Regency Power. Houndstooth. Regal lizard. Amber Rose (code) Send space wines idle while. Send fine lagers ever. Wide unreasonable suit. Whining Mayor (a fake). Transocean signed Captain martyr send Iris signal and help run. Green lemon patron. Help cider. More Scotch. Send universal maroon. Send cricket bats. Junior Navy. Herringbone ten. Aqua fifty-five. Mum's own velvet. Boys' Own Paper. Clips. Flaps. Mumps. Boats. Beds. Too many pink and maroon and magnolia. Signed on China graffito "Joe." Yes, bone China (personal). Oxbone handshake. Glum Mayors. Waders up to the bum. Finnegan's Hall. Byron's Hyde Park roadrunner under the arch. Ship how many freights away Tuesday? Too many. All way back home. Please send tees, shutters, flaxens, needles, tocsins, suds, pumps, raglans, botanicals, turquoise acetate, tire valves,

champagne crepe pantshifts, butter melange, Salem witch house, glyres, bloares, mweers, alps, public gardens. Please send elephant leather chukkas, braised partridge, carryall patch pocket loop-through blendpouch in a variety of stoles. Please send everything: happy roses of life (dames) need instant comfort. Send crocus (for my Japanese juniorette). Yellow pimiento, chili turtleneck for La Vida brava. Send also a message to Carlyle. Solid state. Chef cleft chief ten. Annuity wear poplin top quality premium impact liqueur batiste accelerator tourist accessories and mineral oil. Send. Send. Send send. Sendesend. Send us the other end. Send us all the whiskey.

20. Gryphon rends slipson two piece pioneer. Wave checks a gonerful went. Fully lined savings bake clam tide. Climate is always holy here in Rum. Roses of life come out like flags to welcome police stranger. You can't go wrong with our guard. You add accessories toptop create. Dreamy glassass boats over the ride you fishface. Him boss vanna lighterage. Bovers. Oxers. Beefteas. Stews. Dead hightides climate Duggle Stone Club. Pantry party in the wastelands of Mugg. Up went ten rebels through the viewfinders without flash. Won checks overwhelming barques. Cutty-life still-Sark clambake in editor's home. Much president leads quintet. (Couplet under the bed.) Red forefathers wet the tent. Feeble glare of sportside landing. Why pay extra money for a beach? Deliver big color in sixty flats. $160 model Polaroid second nun. Bishops coming from Cromwell strand. Boston tippety bishop struggles with his finder: doesn't like the view (Poles). Poles apart sighs ace in the cradle. Hot five smokes way over the sea: a five funneled Olympic fights to a draw. Sails over into the mistbergs. Transistorized it makes blackwhite shutterpiece. Shudder

the mudder the fugger under the lugger (seas). Pained spirit of Savoys, meetings, messings, pressings, lavers. MY BONNIE LIES OVER THE OCEAN WITH NEON SCRIPTURES AND SHE IS SENDING PLATES (Mates).
Awright, give it another ten.

21. She is sending me pigeons from Trafalgar panels and stained with colors she is all stranded there. Oh where? Down into the tunnels to find her. Endless are the awaited trains. Gone there. She is sending herself in painted emblems and delicate stained glass. Virgin Mother of lilylight and lost nun of the infirmary nightlight. I go run for the vanished nurse in the subway tunnels of every night.

22. They the cronies are sending spites. Make sure the payers get their plates. Best deliver the bountiful weights to cash songsters. Stripe contours pop colors redsquares and bluestills and greensails. Sweet juleps mend us on our Virginia ways. Sweetmints under the old banktank. Pops out the window and snores a curse over Bank Street: "You come too late and I'll call the police." They the cronies are having a party of twists. Pairs of precious emblems in the windowsights. Why pay extra money for the one on the left? Walking and waking in tropical ranges: two exposure tricolor delivery in the middle of stage. Rectangles and monochromes. Segments and inner faces media mean. Masmass celebrate the wonderful Name. Oils recently placed in sink. Block letouts. Blank letups. Bodyfits under tub.

23. A group of acrylics. Stasis. Sepsis. Cityscapes (cloax, cloax). The bird on the revolving bridge and the watcher on the ravening turntable. Elias with his Polaroid filming the fun. Sit back and stoplooklisten. Under $160. Why pay

more? Gong bundles and secret cameras into uncle tunnel. Down forum drummers into the sun and back into dark next to same cloax. Cloax Max. Circus mum. Palladium hills and the Hippodrum. Vaudeville mums in scanty parallax. All beautiful colors come up in sixty seconds. Still life Dixie postrace march like a mooncolumn advancing into shape. SHE IS SENDING ME ALL HER PAINS and doves her titty posters and contours. Virgins of victory weep their late lights alone lost nights with stills styles and tiny alarms. Waits. The patients liewake lates. Playing the bells until they all vanish down a hole in a carton of smokes.

O RISE AGAIN YOU VACANT SQUARES PIPE TONES
ACROBATIC BARBERS
TAUPES ARE NOW IN ALL THE MOLE GAMES
WINNING THE DIMMEST MIDNIGHT CEERS

Change the flame to number eight. Dreamy glass box will benefit the same. He sleeps wailing for a mate. Famous Tom is drowsing under a weight.

24. Look out mumper lookout to shore. Coonsails! Conmix! Katzenjobber Picnics! Yoyo Silver rushing into the cop-shops. Tonmix riding into places of ownership. Momma Mudder for less than you'd pay. She has a Zeiss under her left and stores information. She has a viewfinder and finds the shapes. Can fashion be considered an investment?

25. THE NORTH AS EVERYBODY KNOWS IS VERY NORD. It is aquilonic.

26. Gare du. Money for Egypt. Mountains of armor way down in Old Cairo where the Virgin blesses Copts and complains about the Holy Spaces. Visit Egypt with Thomas

Mock. Yoyo Lompoc rushing into doubt. They both deliver big. Gare du Garcon. Nasty Nordweapons flame over Suzy Canal.

27. Nordsee chowder. Long shower past Ostende. Shimmer summer. Trawl away over rocking Dutchland. Sick as Dover all over the sea is frailest passenger swooning for the rails. (The missus can't take it.) (Well, keep her under a bed for Class' sake! Keep her under glass for the Sea's sake! Save her glassass for the British viewsem.)

28. Taupes are winning all the cheers this summer. Why pay more for the one that is less? If you add one more accessory you can toptop the funnelbox. You can smell the smokes all the way to Crete. Weeds out of London trawl: Gravesend way. Serious Kent. Reedy showers. Seedy springs. Conrad hunter lives over the beach: hunts editions. Captain Rugby seems unfamiliar at landlubber tea. Major John with a field-size parallax captures the hunter. Funnelhouse sees with twenty eyes. Madmen betting again on the same walking kettle. Kettle's Yard where the paintings are. Funnelhouse meanwhile views with Mafia pot. You can smell the deadly visions all the way to Skete. You can't go wrong in a Skete.

29. North is LNER wending off to Scotch Nero's in the dark. Aberdeen puddings and cobbles. Scotch fisheries. Lake kipperies. The Loch Mess Mumps. The Nordsee haggis. Cuthbert is on his rock warmed by the noses of seals. Hilda on the Hilltower, Bede at his desk, Caedmon in the pub, and Grace sings all her loudest alarms for Old King Cole.

30. Bridgelost. Bridewell. Basewall. Bardbell. Next to St. Andrews. Nord is Forth. Bluegreen aquilons. Walking in a misty season to wink of water. Lighters crafted like jewelry. Pickets like a rave. Cobbles under the castle of a lost queen. Nowhere to assemble in sombre lanes. George comes out briefly in pale sun. He shines on his post. George is sundown's Rex. Crimson boxes of deliverup. Foghorn tempo with gulls. Live whitey, rule the frames. Live whiskey on a thousand clippers.

31. Weeds black sound along gulls foot part waste p:ce foot way humming iron bridge. Begin again the light of lemons in the little mother doors (Lawrence). Mines are Nord. The mine smokes blue. The minesweeper. Shimmer summer the Nordling tree. Minereader. Coal from under the sea. Offside, you lemon!

32. Speaking of famous drinks there might be a lot more and there is.

33. O bell of blue flame from under the mind. Less than human phones. Celtic masters leave aboard the barcraft. Tell it all to delicate feelers (you ought to see with those ears!) Confessions into the eyes of flowers. Foxgloves and bluebells. Telling it to the elves' eyes, the diamond dews of Uxbridge Foxbridge and Harrow. Sweet blue morning of Harrow (Easter) from the Church and down there is Elaine's house. I confess it to the bluebells. You ought to speak to the elms O browneyed Elaine. We were bluebells to one another on the river. The great grey serious river of Nothing.

55

34. Speaking of famous words. The Irish singers whirl the gaudy spokes of Bejaysus all over the Isles of Man Skye and Orkney. There Ezechiel comes in a flaming hearse. He rides his own red monument and announces his swords. Wheels, wings of Merkabah. Flaming Ottomans straight out of Dublin. The jeweled teeth of a heavenly contraption. Come ye Evangels to the coasts of Nord.

35. Run run Ezechiel you are on probation!

36. Top the funnel charnel at the police's corner. The spanky wink. The redred. The walky talk. The phenomenon feeler. The top regarder. The bump on the boss. The ozone of gasometers. Eyeshots and droplet pix. Cunning exposures of fun on the run. Nicked in the nakt. Dressing in the Cadillac. Found in the act. Seeming letters and postals of George in the milky sun. Millways. King of the postbus. Comes with a Gainsborough and puts a pillarbox under the tree. I have drops in my eyes and can't see the pictures. Stunsun Newmarket morning. I can't see the starters because I am gated again. Gated in Bridge Street with a pillar of postals. Shred my letters and feed them to the birds. Stunsun Newmarket morning is wide wide all over. Bookies in the lane. Topfunner Newmocker news. Radios and signs. RAF gleamers. Cries of lonely Auden there in the heights. Lincoln fens are for the airmen. I sit alone under the mornings of Cambridge pylons and watch fliers. Icarus falls.

37. Catch forties. The Millways' Tale told to an autobus. Running home from Chesterton by night among the fences. Stunsun and it is another morning. Sunday down by the boatless river. Goldilights of Northmorning see telltale

Maundies colder and older. Gold February tells Millways'
boat to spill amid a calm. Tall stands of Twickenham cap-
tains. Baroque pieties of a fine Anglican. Loves' labour lost
in Twickenham garden.

38. Winner take all Mondays. Climates. Emblem. Sur-
plices. Twinkling garden vision precision eyebeams strung
on a string. (Get thee to an eyedoctor.) Excise manage-
ment pouring into Pauls with innocent faces cleam. Strike
out Mazdas of John Dean oh great dark grinning death-
shirt John dumbstruck subway under a guilty city! (The
bombers come!)

39. Stained stained to Henley Thames we go to tame the
water with our butterflies.

40. Famous John is inventing you a trap with his agents.
Old effigy with Anglican sabres. That turning stair goes up
to a stone tiger. Tiger burns with his own secret fright.
Sinners are betting on a walking kettle of eyes. Tiger tiger
burning in the bay escapes double vision. Lettertrap for
old Posthumus. (*Eheu fugaces* said our clock in Rye. The
clock at Fletcher's.) Oho fliers posthumus oho the airmail
letters flip over and glide away. Butterfly papers. Ten a
penny prayers. Guarded petitions pouring into Pauls with
evident vital claims. Torn out of a lovelorn long summer
in Elmhurst (Ruthie had a friend). Simplicissimus (not
funny). With a lovesick butterfly (*Fugaces*). Sing it all
aloud. Sing sang sung song Cleo to the welkin! The musi-
cal Nord is forever aquilonic.

41. Sing a song to Momma Mudder. Winner has all the
grey climates. Millways' gone home in the rigging of

misted eyebeams. Baroque summers of hear my song O Thames (flow sweetly til I end). It was light week in Lograire and we saw it in the relatives' field and the way of the world is bent. The Edisons blink. Blink at a cardinal winner out in sportsdale. Make sure the prayers all get to their right place. Stranded in the sun. Sane song sing sang sun! Time tongue tokens of lovelorn trancer. Shimmering Thames by Westminster and under the Savoy. The young hotel is quiet as a nun. Welkin sunstruck welkin sunstruck welkin. Lobsang rivers of Lammermoor. Long-lasting limes. Stained in tunnels claimed by the all seeing master-funnels. Very funny coming into light: sinners all chasing a five legged kettle. Butterfly traffic ten a penny. My prayers are all torn out of the mourning paper. Sing sang song to lucky welkin! Sing sang sun tone (think of a magazine). Suntown Cleotone sang song in downing sun (a Loma) An-cleo-tony. The phone song sung alone at dawn. Prayer is vast (the moaning paper!) the waste blue sky. Gone cleo is my clear tone welkin. I die praising!

42. Hello Argus yes this is Argus police please I have to report a walking kettle yes every day sinners active in every street. Send agents teargas bazooka mace to slightly broken home of double trouble. Run to our tumble here at Connie's Inn. Signed: Boston.

43. Voice of a prayer lip stumbles in gross assent.
HELLO AGENTS THIS IS RELIGION CALLING FOR HELP.
Send Argus to command another. Try that second election. Seize another paramilitary chance. Well-meaning prayer lip again fumbles message. IS GOD IN KENT?

44. Light tower panic in election night view semblance of sheeted type on garden prowl (ten are bit by bats).

Commotion in the mixture. Coonselves permit a dilemma. Loud are the batteries. Favorites all dead. Blossoms insane night with Edison flakes. All red screams Connie in raided bed. Connie Mamma is ahead of dusk (in her sheets). She goes off with lights around her head (the final Regina). Moral redress calls to arms: types explain (rest room in Albuquerque). My Connie lies over the ocean with the doublespread. My Connie is back in the North with pillows under her head. Dramas begin again in Elmhurst. Mum is the laundress.

45. Judge hold hands. Slow door closes in defence. Maladies of innocence! Protect the lives of your local Mafia.

46. When I sat down and wept by Sandy river the city was filled with Mafia passengers landing from the air. O the light came down and wept on the runways. Tiger burning in the weeds escapes double vision. George's geography is all trouble with spies. Nord is the red of Scotland Yard. I stood by the weighing machine in a room so bare so bare. Bare as St. James' Infirmary the room my baby there. My Bonnie was in the far north laid out on a long white table.

47. Mister Justice with frosty eye say too many little legs are going by (the kettle of Hieronymus Bosch). Scary kettle of drugs. Knottypot. Right dress! Squads of drunken bottles all over the yard. Marching vessels. Yes bottles have eyes springs scents visions. Order cubes. Expand senses. Recall movers. Mister Judge with frosty eye view too many senses walking by. Stop that kettle it looks so funny walking at a trot. All the trees walking (like men). The wallpaper has eyes and moves watching. Mister Judge with frosty eye see too many movies going by (on the same

wall). Bottles with hips. Oh mercy, jugs with hands! Little gleamy unkind jars. Phials stick out tongues. A crow flies out of the pitcher. Judge Doublethink condemns an icecube. Restores senses, scents, visions, touches, tastebuds. Stop that kettle walking up the wall on all fours stop those swinging flocks of flocons. STOP THAT PAPER STOP THAT FLASK. STOP ACK ACK STOP FLAK. Too late. Every instrument is moving!

48. Geography is in trouble all over Lograire. Rape of maps by military arm. Judgments fly out of crowsnests all around prison. Points. Pens. Bibbed Parson Calvin bites pot with conviction. Pastor Fingerbone moves jug and troubles the oil. Points to grease foul well name (famous scrambled). Pastor Crowfoot bugs a Delta home. Officer Foulball comes in daddywagon to end Black War of Astoria. Is assailed on Northern Blvd. Pastor Wallpaper does vile sums in the toilets. Father Topknot works for bishops in crowsnest surrounding slum. Performs the deadly operation. Removes another building. All the fractions are in jail being complimented by sermons.

49. Dear Togs. I have chosen electric life with spades. The lines here are almost new. Home is underwater now. Conscience is a bronco well busted. Memory secured by electronic tape. Gunshots on the glassy swamps of night. Uniforms wade under willows calling to the dead.

50. So Christ went down to stay with them Niggers and took his place with them at table. He said to them, "It is very simple much simpler than you imagine." They replied, "You have become a white man and it is not so simple at all."

II

"There is a grain of sand in Lambeth which Satan cannot
        find."
There is a child of God in the sacred cellar undressing
        Louise.
My little brother is climbing all over Catherine.
There is a seed of light in us that cannot be bought
        by Grove Press.
With Pat by the boulders in late afternoon the sailboats did
        not see it.
Tall elms meditate all night and the big dog looks
        into the back seat
The daughters of Schenley approach and withdraw.
They have to giggle.
We sink quietly into naked water where Satan cannot find
        any sand whatever
But where the condoms of others will float in full view
On New Year's morning.

There is a grain of sand in boarding school down
        the long hall
And giant elms cover the cricket field with shadow
I am photographed in an embarrassed collar
My Jerusalem is wide awake with watch fiends
I am searched and investigated by baying bitches
I am a grain of fear in village churches.

There is a pebble of Jerusalem in Ealing
Listens to the everlasting piano in the next home

On spring nights when there is no sleeping
Because the rivers of life are wide awake
And a child must die into manhood
On the cricket field

There is a grain of sand in Lambeth which Satan
        cannot find
While deep in the heart's question a shameless light
Returns no answer.

III. THE RANTERS AND THEIR PLEADS
(London)

1. *Sessions of Gaole delivery held in the Old Bayley the 18, 19, and 20 of this instant January, 1651*
". . . She commends the Organ, Viol, Symbal and Tonges in Charterhouse Lane to be heavenly musick; she tosseth of her glasses freely and comendeth there is no heaven but the pleasures she injoyeth upon earth; she is very familiar at first sight and danceth the Canaries at the sound of a hornpipe."

(*The Routing of the Ranters, 1650*)

2. Met at a tavern
   The David and Harp in Moor Lane
   Sang: "Ram me dam me!"
   And other blasphemies
   To the tune of the Psalms
   Alleged that "Ram"
   Was another name for "God"
   When about to be arrested
   Took up a candle
   Looked in all the corners
   "hunting for his sins"
   And said (so brazen)
   "he found not one."
   Apprehended, examin'd, arraign'd in Old Bayley
   Was sent to Bridewell to beat hemp
   With six companions

Who had danced at supper
Tearing a piece of beef
With damnable opinions
Prancing to the viol
In Adamitic orgies
Calling one another:
"Fellow creature"!

3. GANGRAENA: A CATALOGUE OF ERROURS

"Every creature is an efflux from God
And shall return into God again
As a drop is in the ocean."

"If God be all things then he is sin and wickednesse;
and if he be all things then he is this Dog, this Tobacco
Pipe, he is in me and I am in him, I have heard some
say, blaspheming . . ."

"*. . . A deep mystery and great ocean
Where there is no casting anchor
No sounding the bottome.*"

Item: "That there shall be a generall Restauration
wherein all men shall be reconciled to God and saved."
Impious doctrine.

They dishonour and cry downe the Churche!

"I could relate also other errours as that:

IF A MAN WERE STRONGLY MOVED BY THE SPIRIT TO
KILL OR TO COMMIT ADULTERY AND UPON PRAYING

HE SHOULD DO IT!"

An eye and ear witness
A more true and fuller discovery
Of the Doctrine of those men

4. "Now is the Creature damm'd and ramm'd into its
    only Center
   Into the bowels of still Eternity, its Mother's womb
   There to dwell forever unknown
   This and this only is the 'damnation'
   So much terrifying the creature
   In its dark apprehensions . . ."

5. GRAND IMPOSTURES ABOMINABLE PRACTISES GROSS DECEITS
   LATELY SPREAD ABROAD AND ACTED IN THE COUNTY OF
   SOUTHAMPTON.

   . . . M. Stubs a late fellow Ranter.

6. Distempered with sickness
   Distracted in brain
   Thou has left off to read.

   ". . . and that makes thee to be such a wathercock,
   such a well without water, such a wandering star as
   thou art, such a cloud tost to and fro with a tempest,
   because thou hast no steady rule to steer by or to fix
   thee to any one point, but only the whistling, multi-
   farious fancies and foolish figments of thine own aiery
   brain and inconstant spirit . . ."

"A people so dronish that the whole course of their life
is but one SCENE OF SOTTISHNESS."

(The Ranters' Religion)

7. An Abominable Ranter, Jacob Bauthemly, wrote that
the Devil and Hell were "the Dark Side of God" and
wrote it while in the army. Therefore he was punished
by being burned through the tongue. He was after-
ward found with Quakers and Ranters in Leicester-
shire spreading his foul sayings and abominations:

"O God what shall I say thou art when thou cans't
not be named
For if I say I see thee it is nothing but thy seeing
of thyself . . .

"Nay, I see that God is in all creatures,
Man and Beast, Fish and Fowle,
And every green thing from the highest cedar to the
ivey on the wall;
And that God is the life and being of them all . . .

"As all things were let out of God:
So shall they all give up their Being, life and
happiness
Unto God again
Though the clothing dissolve and come to nothing
Yet the inward man still lives . . .

"I find that where God dwells and is come
And hath taken men up and rapt them up
in the Spirit;
There is a new heaven and a new earth

And my heaven is to have my earthly and dark
Apprehensions of God to cease
And to live no other life than what Christ
Spiritually lives in me . . .

"Sin is the dark side of God but God is not
    the author of sin
Nor does he will it. Sin being a nullity, God cannot
    be the author of it."

8. PROOFS EXAMINATIONS DECLARATIONS
   INDICTMENTS AND CONVICTIONS
   ARRAIGNMENT AND TRYALL
   DAMNABLE AND DIABOLICAL OPINIONS
   DETESTABLE LIVES AND ACTIONS

Late prodigious pranks and unparalleled deportments
Notorious corrupting and disordering of society
"Withal they enjoyned a cursed doctrine of
    LIBERTINISM
Which brought them to all abominable filthiness
    of life:
They say that for a man to be tyed to one woman
Or one woman to one man
Is a fruit of the curse.

SMOKE OF THE BOTTOMLESS PIT
VENTED AND ACTED IN ENGLAND.

9. A Way for Suppression of the obscene licentious and
impious Practices used by Persons under Pretense of
Liberty and Religion.

10. They teach that there is neither heaven nor hell
    But what is in man.

    They do not apprehend any wrath
    To be in God.

    I saw a letter that one of them writ to a friend of his
    And at the bottom of the letter he writ thus:
    "From Heaven and Hell or from Deptford
    In the first yeare of my reconciliation to my Selfe."

    Then God does not hate? Not even sin?
    So heaven and hell are in Deptford, Woolwich,
                Battersea and Lambeth?

    Burn him through the tongue!

IV. KANE RELIEF EXPEDITION

1

Morning came at last
The storm over we sighted
Quiet mountains green and
Silver Edens
Walls of an
Empty country—Near?
(We were deceived—30 miles at least)

You can tell when Sunday comes
Everything on shipboard
Quieter
        icebergs like churches
Slow sailing gifts
           visions
A sailor intoned
An Anglican hymn

"One iceberg on our port bow
Resembled a lady dressed in white
Before her shrine"
(Dazzling whiteness
        gemm'd with blue-green)
"In the attitude of prayer"

"As if some magician, etc. . . ."

"Gifts—visions"

A huge berg between us
And the green shore.
"As we were gazing it grounded and the shock caused one
end of it to fall over upon the other and both turned over.
A terrible sight. Crashed like thunder. Spray flew mast-
high"

Then whales came
And played around us all day.

2

Black parapets
Of Disko conjured
Out of cold rain
Something like a sentry box
On a tall summit

A boat shot out
Suddenly produced
From behind that rock
Came for us
With six eskimos
And Lieut. Saxtroph
Of the Danish army.

Our pilot took over
Headed straight for the rock
A crack in the cliff
Ninety yards wide
Secret basin land-
Locked dark
All stone straight up

Two thousand feet
Into the rain
Not a spot of green
I inquir'd where to
Look for the town
He pointed to
Twelve cabins.

Then kayaks all around us
Offered fish for sale
You could obtain
A duck for a bisquit

"The Lieutenant had been in the wars between Denmark
and Schleswig Holstein; he spoke English very well and
during our stay at Lievly done everything in his power to
make our time pass pleasantly. He was a splendid dancer
and sang the national songs of his country with much
spirit."

3

We climbed to a graveyard
High on the wet rock
There bodies sleep in crevices
Covered with light earth then stones
Some were sailors from England
And America
Now asleep
In this black tower
Over Baffin's Bay
Waiting, waiting
In endless winter.

We left them to their sleep
Ran down to meet the living girls.

"I would have given almost anything for a daguerrotype
of that room. Voices soft and clear eyes light blue or hazel.
Not one bad tooth. Their hair is all combed up to the top
of the head and twisted into a knot and tied with ribbons,
red for the unmarried, blue for the married ones. Jumper
or jacket lined with finely dressed deerskin trimmed with
fur and a band of ribbon. The most beautiful part of their
dress is the pantaloons of spotted seal, very soft, with an
embroidered stripe down the front which says: 'ready for
marriage.'"

We called for a Polka. The band
"Struck up Camptown Races we had taught them
The previous night"
Seizing our partners
We all commenced

Better dancing
I never saw at home.

"The space between the pants and boots is filled with a
legging of linen or muslin edged and lined with deerskin.
They were all scrupulously clean."

4

75° N. Melville Bay
July 29.
"A conical island in a bay of ice to starboard. It is the
Sugar Loaf island of whalers. It tells that on rounding

the headland now in sight (Wilcox Point) we shall see the
far-famed Devil's Thumb the boundary of dreaded Mel-
ville Bay."

July 30.
"Toiling slowly through the leads with plenty of bear
tracks around us."

July 31.
"A good lead opening. Towed twelve miles. The much
talked of Devil's Thumb is now in sight. It appears to be
a huge mass of granite . . . Here begins Melville Bay."

Bay of ice and gales
Grave of whalers
Where "in one disastrous year the whaling fleet
Lost twenty-eight sail."

From the Devil's Thumb northward
Vast glacier
"One of the manufactories
From whence the huge icebergs
Are given off"

Fifty miles wide.

8 days driven to and fro
By masses of ice.
                    Waiting
To be crushed
"All provisions on deck
Ready for a run
At a moment's warning."

The bark was thrown over on her beam ends
Our batteau lashed to the bulwark
Was ground to atoms
In a couple of minutes.

"All hands on the qui vive for a smash."

(Must we go 200 miles over ice
Dragging our boats
To Upernavik?)

Finally clear of pack ice on the 13th
We stood for Cape York
Red snow on the rocks. Open water
Finally out
Of Melville Bay!

5

Cape Alexander

Here K. promised to leave a cairn
And a bottle with a clear account of his proceedings
To tell us his intended course
Instead
A small mound
A homeopathic vial containing a mosquito
Covered with cotton
A small piece of cartridge paper
With the letters "OK" written on it
As if with the point of a bullet.

6

78° N. Cape Haterton and Etah

Two Indians on a rock
Like an owl's cry
Signalling

"We landed and found a village of tents in a valley with a
lake of fresh water. A large glacier over the edge of which
a cataract was pouring into the lake. Grass almost knee
deep, full of flowers. Indians in dogskins and the skins of
birds collected around us and examin'd our firearms with
the greatest attention."

"We soon found unmistakable signs of K.'s party having
been there. Knives and cutlery bearing the mark of the
Green River works. Pewter cups and part of a microscope.
Preserved meat and pemmican cans, baking pans, forks,
spoons, a piece of a shirt with the initials H.B., spools of
cotton marked N. York, curtain material, the top rail of a
berth, red velvet and an ivory handled carving knife . . ."

"By signs they gave us to understand that the vessel had
been crushed in the ice. This they done by taking a clay
pipe and crushing it between their hands."

"They pointed to a child and made signs
That K. was a small man
Bald and without whiskers."

O hairless Kane
Lost in ice

How long gone?
They do not understand
Time
But he cured
One of their children.

They catch birds on the rocks by means of nets
Eat the birds raw
Give anything for a knife.

That ivory handled carving knife
Probably stolen.

7

Possession Bay

"Moonlight among the ice presents a scene that none but
those who have sail'd in Arctic regions can form any con-
ception of. It glances from the floe ice with a blinding
glare and gives the icebergs the appearance of mountains
of light.

"Light streaming through a tall archway in a berg
Like scenes in the showy fairy pieces
At the theaters."

8

Pond's Bay

Rookery of loons
"Greatest sight of bird doings"
Cliffs terraced notched every projection
Covered

Thousands
Wheeling over us in moon-
Light so tame
You could knock them down with an oar

Deafening.

"We entered a cave at the foot of the cliff and found it
filled with young loons and gulls."

So we shot 500 weighing 1172 lbs.

9

Sept 4th 1855

Midnight. Gale.

"Get up Dr. we are rushing down on an iceberg."

As I reached the deck
We crashed.

A huge iceberg
Four times as high as the mast
Overhangs our ship
More of the same
Starboard
White mass
Driven head on we
Beat against it
Bows staved in jib

Boom carried away we
Recoil swing star-
Board beam smashes
Into small end of ice-
Berg quarterboat in splinters
All bulwarks driven in
Cathead bumpkins and the rest
Gone
         Wind
Swirling around angle of ice
Like a hurricane
Rush for boats driven back:
"We fired minute guns but the gale was so high the noise
of crashing ice so great the steamer could not hear us . . ."

(The account ends here. Both expeditions reached safety.)

EAST

EAST

LOVE OF THE SULTAN

A SLAVE
CUTS OFF HIS OWN HEAD
AFTER A LONG SPEECH
DECLARING HOW MUCH
HE LOVES THE SULTAN

A QUAINT OLD ASIAN CUSTOM

LOVE
OF
THE
S U L T A N !

81

I. EAST WITH IBN BATTUTA

1. Cairo 1326

Cloisters (khanqahs) of Darvishes
Built by aristocrats
Have silver rings on their doors
The mystics sit down to eat
Each from his private bowl
Each drinks
From his own cup
They are given
Changes of clothing
And a monthly allowance
On Thursday nights
They are given sugar
Soap and oil
For their lamps
And the price of a bath.

In the great cemetery
They build chambers
Pavilions
Hire singers
To chant the *Koran*
Day and night among the tombs
With pleasant voices.

Convent at Dayr at-Tin:
A piece of the Prophet's
Wooden basin with the pencil
With which he applied kohl

The awl
With which he sewed his sandals
Bought by the founder
For a hundred thousand dirhams.

2. *Syria*

Ma'arra and Sarmín: towns
Of abominable Shi'ites
Who hate the Ten Companions
And every person called Omar

In Sarmín (where scented soap
Is made and exported
To Damascus and Cairo)
These heretics so hate the Ten
They will not even say "Ten"
Their brokers at auctions
When they come to "ten"
Say "Nine-plus-one"

One day a faithful Turk
At one of their markets
Heard the broker call "Nine-plus-one"
He went for him with a club, shouting
"You bastard, say TEN!"

"Ten with a club"
Wept the broker.

3. *The Nusayris*

These heretics hate all true believers and when ordered by
      the Sultan
To build mosques build them far from their homes
Keep asses and cattle in them let them fall into disrepair.

If a true believer coming from another country
Stops in a ruined mosque and sings the call to prayer
The infidels say: "Stop braying,
We will bring you a little hay."

Once a stranger came to the Nusayris and told them he was
       the Mahdi
He promised to divide Syria among them
Giving each one a city or a town.
He gave them olive leaves and said:
"These will bring you success. These leaves
Are warrants of your appointment."

They went forth into city and town
And when arrested, each said to the Governor:
"The Imám al-Mahdi has come. He has given me
          this town!"

The Governor would then reply: "Show me your warrant"

Each one then produced his olive leaves
And was flogged.

So the stranger told the heretics to fight:
"Go with myrtle rods," he said
"Instead of swords. The rods
Will turn to swords at the moment of battle."

They entered a town on Friday when the men were
       at the mosque.
They raped the women and the Muslims
Came running out with swords
And cut them to pieces.

News was sent to the capital by carrier pigeon.
        The Governor
Moved out with an army. Twenty thousand heretics
Were slaughtered. The rest hid in the mountains.
They offered one dinar per head if they were spared.
This news went by pigeon to the Sultan
Who said: "Kill them."

But the General
Said these people could be useful
Working on the land
And their lives were spared.

4. Mecca

"The Meccans are very elegant and clean in their dress, and
most of them wear white garments, which you always see
fresh and snowy. They use a great deal of perfume and
kohl and make free use of toothpicks of green arák-wood.

"The Meccan women are extraordinarily beautiful and very
pious and modest. They too make great use of perfumes to
such a degree that they will spend the night hungry in
order to buy perfumes with the price of their food.

"They visit the mosque every Thursday night, wearing
their finest apparel; and the whole sanctuary is saturated
with the smell of their perfume. When one of these women
goes away the odour of the perfume clings to the place
after she has gone."

5. *Isfahan*

In Isfahan the fair
Surrounded by orchards
(Apricots and quinces
Pears and melons)
The people out-do one another
In banquets
"In the preparation for which
They display all their resources"
One corporation entertained another with viands
Cooked over candles
"The guests returned the invitation
And cooked their viands with silk."

6. *Delhi*

In the Sultan's apartments
I saw a *Júgí*
Sitting in midair
I fell in a faint
They had to give me a drink
To revive me

And there he was
Still sitting in midair
His companion
Took a sandal from a bag
Beat it on the ground
Til it rose in the air
All by itself and poised
Over the floating one

86

And it began hitting him
On the back of the neck
Until he floated down
And landed.

"I would tell them to do something else,"
Said the Sultan, "If I did not fear
For your reason."

7. *Calicut*

Chinese vessels at anchor in the harbor
One of the largest in the world. Malabar
Coast of ginger pepper spice
Four decks with cabins saloons
Merchants of Canton Sumatra
Ceylon stay locked in cabins
With wives and slave girls
Sailors bring their boys to sea
Cultivate salads and ginger
In wooden vats

In Calicut I missed my boat
To China and my slave
Girls were all stolen by the King
Of Sumatra and my companions
Were scattered over China
Sumatra and Bengal

When I saw what had happened
I sailed for the Maldives
Where all the inhabitants
Are Muslims

Live on red fish lightly cooked
Or smoked in palmleaf baskets
It tastes like mutton

These natives wear no pants
Only aprons
Bathe twice a day
Use sandalwood and do not fight
Their armor is prayer.

II. EAST WITH MALINOWSKI

TUPUSELEIA

We tack into the lagoon
Shipping water I am ready
To throw up

           "Having
The time of my life!"

("He feeling good feeling
Good!" The Filipino giggled
As the passenger
Staggered through the club car
To vomit.)

The time of my life
In a double canoe
With the policeman
And another savage
On the aerial WC
Wrapped in a coxswain's cloak

Kurukuru grass—like rye straw
Golden houses dip their thatch
At high tide

Stimmung—desertion
(Death in Venice)

Dark inside
Bronze bodies appear
At the doors
(Do not shoot
Til you see the whites of their eyes)

"From time to time firm breasts stick out"
(Fear of pointed objects)

Kurukuru stacks (houses)
"Dip their long thatch beards
In the water"
(Morning)
But at night (lowtide)
"I urinated from a height of 13 feet."

Morning again gentle hills
Sprawling spidery trees.
"I evacuated straight into the sea
From a privy above the water"

Then we talked of sun and moon
And the causes of things
On the way to Port Moresby
And McCann's Hotel
Sherry and the gramophone
Icy beer and
                    ". . . that woman
Vulgar beyond endurance."

III.   CARGO SONGS

1. Sir William MacGregor
   Representative of Her Majesty the Queen
   Saw the Paramount Chief enthroned
   On a high platform
   Went up and seized him by the hair
   Dragged him to the ground
   Placed himself firmly in the seat of honor:
   "No one shall sit higher in Papua than I."

2. The anthropologist lay low
   Shivered under the hot compress
   Read Bronte and pissed black
   When the wind blew off the sea
   He thought he felt better
   Seemed to hear the bell-charm of St. Martin's
   And Strand traffic humming in his head
   Lay thinking of French chophouses in Soho
   Of anything in fact
   But Trobriand Islanders and coral gardens
   Even his intimate fantasies were far away
   In Russia: Rasputin: a convenient system!
   "How wicked I am," sighed the anthropologist,
   "I need more quinine
   And no one shall sit higher in Trobriand than I."

3. Meanwhile four natives must hang
   Each in a different village
   To impress the population

The proceedings throughout
Were watched with great interest
By chiefs and a number
Of other natives
All appeared impressed
By the solemnity.

4. Hatedevil missionary has a waxen smell
   Long narrow trousers find their way to hell
   Rams chickens forbidden Kava and the vices
   Of a rivergod seen between trees
   An old man with a forgettable name
   Lights volcano nine.
   The Captain notes odd behavior and shivers.

5. Even though
   The anthropologist is laid low
   There is still nobody higher.

6. After this a native from the North side of Milne Bay
   Possessed by a tree-spirit
   Warned of giant waves
   All must throw away
   Matches, knives, white men's tools
   Destroy houses kill all pigs
   Withdraw inland
   Wearing only long narrow leaves
   "To show entire repudiation of the white man."

7. On the following Sunday the missionary noted with
   surprise that his congregation now consisted only of a
   few children. He learned that the villagers were all in
   the hills, expecting the return of the dead. He pushed

inland without further delay. He found all the men of the village sitting in tense silence. His cordial greeting met with no reply.

8. But the missionary had come prepared:

"I had in my wallet a long thin stick of trade tobacco, a delicacy very much prized by these people, and as I was sitting in the doorway of the Chief's house I took it out and threw it to some men who were sitting behind me in the dark. Almost before they had time to pick it up it came back and struck me in the ear." (*Rev. Abel*)

9. The whites then made for safety moving fast in small groups to the coast. They reached the boats in time. The dead arrived in the village with a cargo of flashlights.

10. Now there is a black King living in the jungle, Iron, with a stone grey skin. Kanaka Shiva, thirty hands, getting ready to shake another mountain. The sky rains magic fire from Black Master. Burning kerosene eats up the villages. Ancestors come with canned meat new suits and plenty of rifles. "A small ring of dancers. Two dancers facing each other with raised drums."

11. But the anthropologist
    Lives with memories
    "The walk with Miss Nussbaum
    In a glacier blue outfit
    The persistent longing
    For mother."

12. *Ein ganz eigentümlich Vorgang.*

Blackfela Catholic Mambu sprinkled their organs with
    holywater
And remained unmarried like a mission sister.
He fed the people with rice that had arrived secretly
    by air.
The church burned down when the Father was home
    in Germany and this was a sign he said.

13. *Ein undankbares, schweres Missionsfeld* said the Father
    on his return.

14. Meanwhile they had eaten everything. The villages
    seemed unnaturally quiet, "full of natives in
    European dress, sitting very still."

They said their ship had now started from Rome
Bringing fountain pens and the removal
Of mystical penalties.

15. "Famous young couple originates new life." Sign on
    this line.
Be ready for big Blackfela Catholic Steamer:
        Most Sacred Heart of Jesus Ltd
        Turns brown man white
        In a quaking boat
        Full of ancestors
        Speaking in tongues.

But saner elements visited the scientist and told him
    everything.

94

16. Filo a gifted virgin dreamt of God
Who told her what he thought of white people.

17. The anthropologist suffered a fit of nervous aversion
for pointed objects.

18. Filo said God had told her he was sending a truckload
of rifles. One man broke through the fence and nearly
brained the Father with a sea shell. A mission brother
slipped away crossed to the other island to bring the
magistrate and officers. Some rebels got seven years.
Filo returned under police escort. There was only a
mild demonstration though everybody knew some to-
bacco had really fallen from heaven.

19. "I gave them portions of tobacco and they all walked
away without posing long enough for a time exposure.
My feelings toward them: exterminate the brutes."
(*Malinowski*)

20. "Igua massaged me and told me in *delightful* Motu
about murders of white men as well as his fears of
what he would do if I died in that way."

21. But a little wire can take a lot of juice and no man
shall sit higher in Trobriand than I.

IV. PLACE NAMES

Jair son of Manasseh went and seized the encampments
And called them the Encampments of Jair
Nobah went and seized Kenath
With its outlying villages
And called it Nobah
After himself.

                         (*Numbers 32: 41-42*)

1827

D'Entrecasteaux enters the bay
Looks it over
Leaves it with name of his ship:
"Astrolabe Bay."

1871-1883

Baron Nikolai Miklouho-Maclay
(Tibud Maclay)
Comes and goes
Exploring
Recording the language
As a reward for hospitality
Leaves the coast with
His own name:
"Maclay Coast"

To further honor
The place where he landed
He called it "Constantine Harbour"
(Grand Duke Constantine
President of the Imperial Russian Geographical Society
Had paid for the trip.)

1878

Australian gold-prospectors
Put in at Bongu
In the good ship *Dove*
But leave at once
Forgetting to name the place
"Dove Harbor"
But there is a "Dove Point"
A hundred miles up the coast.

1884

Herr Finsch
Representing the Neu Guinea Kompagnie
Hoists the German flag
Over "Bismarck (naturally)
Archipelago" "Kaiser
(Of course) Wilhelmsland"
And last but not least
"Finschhafen."

V. TIBUD MACLAY

Tibud Maclay
Came from the moon in a white ship
Stood without weapons
In a shower of arrows
Sat in a bungalow
Full of remedies cameras optical
Instruments and presents
Walked in the night
With his blue lamp

Tibud Maclay
A culture hero
From the land of figureheads
Inventor of nails mirrors
Melons and paint
Whose servant flew away
Over the horizon
Without wings

Tibud Maclay
With a Swede and an Islander
Blue as a god or ancestor
Warned them there would be
Two kinds of white man
Arriving later
A few good
The rest very bad
Hostile deities

Djamans with firearms
Would rob them of land
Work them under whips
Shoot them if they
Ran away

The people
Took this warning to heart
But could not understand

Soon came Herr Finsch
A decent *Djaman*
Saying he was the brother
Of Tibud Maclay
So they received him gladly
He hoisted his flag over their villages
While they celebrated his coming

Then all the others
Began to arrive
They gave the people two axes
Some paint and matches
And then went into business
Taking over the country.

News travelled all over the islands:
"No end of visitors!
Get ready to entertain!"

VI. SEWENDE (Seven Day)

1. Seven Day is an unknown country where aspirins
   come from
   And pants and axes and corned beef in cans
   It is far beyond the green sea, the white sea, the blue sea
   Past Tokyo North America and Germany
   But in the same general direction
   Far far beyond other countries
   No one has seen this blessed land

   In the center of snow-night-day
   Is a more hidden place
   Even more unknown than Sewende
   The front door of Big Belong
   Who got up very old
   Out of Himself in the beginning
   Left His endless bed in the morning
   And started the Cargo Company
   In which we now offer shares
   To True Believers.

2. Then the dreamer said we must build a large warehouse
   in the bush. We must do everything he said and then
   wait: in a short time the warehouse would be filled with
   cans of meat, aspirins, hydrogen peroxide, soap, razor
   blades, rice, pants, flashlights and everything.

   Then we built the warehouse together. And after that
   the dreamer said we must wash away all our impurities.
   We all drew water and heated it and washed together.

We went in silence to the burial ground. Nobody sang
or danced or said anything. We just sat very still in the
dark waiting for the signal.

At the signal the women took theirs off and we took
ours off and we all began. It was all collected in a bot-
tle with water and poured over the burial place to bring
Cargo.

When the Administration heard about it we had to tear
down the warehouse and carry all the timbers eighteen
miles and throw them in the sea.

3. PRAYER OF KAUM

    written in Whiteman's jail
    where he was killed and went to Paradise
    To see with his own eyes
    Ancestors making Cargo
    To be shipped to the islands
    And see with his own eyes
    Whiteman changing all the labels:

    "O Father Consel you are so sorry
    You are so sorry for us Kanakas.
    You can help us we have nothing no planes
    No jeeps no ships not even hammers not even pants
    Nothing at all because Whiteman
    Steals everything and you are so sorry
    O Father Consel
    Now you send
    Something."

    (So sorry!)

VII. CARGO CATECHISM

1. Here is how it all began. Old Anut made him some man and woman along flowers animals trees fish putem in a garden belong plenty canned beef ricebags (polished) instant coffee, tobacco matches and candybars. Old man and woman no pants and lots of whiskey. Baimbai plenty pekato mekim plenty trabel. Nogut. Old Anut took away all the canned food before they could even find the canopener. Quick lockup garden and hide all the whiskey. You wantem inferno Ol Man Adam? "Suppose you spik: I no got inferno, baimbai you go along IN."

2. Noah was a gutfela so Old Anut showed him how to build a steamer. Make him strongfela talk: get along steamer with plenty Cargo along all animals quick I make him rain longtime no can finish. Noah had a peaked cap white shirt shorts stockings and shoes. The rain came down and Noah rang the bell and off went the steamer with all the animals that's all. Steamer belong plenty canned beef ricebags (polished) instant coffee tobacco matches and candybars. No whiskey. Old Noah always properly dressed. Nix pekato. Nix trabel.

3. Baimbai rain stops and steamer lands in Australia. Old Noah finds a bottle of whiskey lying around Sydney. Bad news for everybody that's all. Noah want'em one drink work him trouble no can finish. One drink takes off shoes. Two drinks takes off the socks. Son Ham belongs Noah watches and laughs when old boy takes off his pants.

For this Ham is deprived of cargo, canned meat, razorblades etc and sent to New Guinea to be a black man. Shem and Japheth remain white, keep the Cargo and remain in Sydney.

4. Ham belong longtime taro gardens in New Guinea without Cargo canned meat razorblades etc but surrounded by friendly satans who produce good crop. Satans promote much dancing and although there is no whiskey they can work pretty good love magic. Plenty trabel but could be a lot worse (inferno). Food however too simple nothing but roots and pig meat none of it canned and no instant coffee, candybars, polished rice, cocacola, etc. Suppose you wanem canned food you better get rid of Satans. HERAUS! RAUSIM SATAN!

5. Whitefellow come along from Sydney to help *rausim satans,* with less dancing and more work also bibles. Trouble with Bible: is *incomplete.* All the instructions about Cargo torn out. Best parts all missing, rewritten by Jews.

6. Correct information. The ancestors are alive and well in the sky immediately above Sydney Australia. Taught and supervised by the God of the Catholics they are putting meat into cans and sending it to New Guinea correctly labelled for the natives. Also flashlights, razorblades, hammers, etc. Plenty for everybody, black and white alike. While the Cargo is at sea the white crew spends all its time changing the labels and readdressing the natives' shipments to planters, missionaries, government officials and policemen. The problem now is how to get Cargo direct without recourse to ships and planes belonging to white men?

7. Jesus Christ is now in Sydney waiting to deliver Cargo to natives without the intervention of white men. He has a steamer and it is all loaded. But he does not yet have the proper clothing. Jesus Christ is waiting in a hotel room for someone to bring him a suit.

8. Word travels fast down the coast. Large gatherings are dispersed by the police. Families are arrested and put in jail because they have arranged bouquets of flowers for the coming of Jesus with the Cargo.

9. In 1940 amid rumors of distant war a local leader in Madang, after two hours of silent prayer, stood up and announced that the King was coming to take over. Another declared that he was the Apostle Paul and had a radio like the Australians.

The one who announced the Advent of the King was immediately arrested but he was released when, after questioning, it became clear that he was not referring to the Germans.

But the people understood why he had been arrested! Henceforth his message was taken very seriously. Flowers were on display everywhere. When those who displayed flowers were arrested, bouquets were made in secret and hidden under baskets. As soon as Jesus appeared with Cargo they would lift up the baskets. Their world would be all flowers.

VIII. JOHN THE VOLCANO

1

I John Frum—Volcano ancestor—Karaperamun
"My Brother here is Joe
Everything is near to me
See us two Joe-Captain: Cockle Shell."

My three sons come down out of my sky
In long robes and jackets
They are invisible to women
Except to Gladys a little girl
My three sons show themselves under the banyan tree
Giving orders to boys and girls who do not understand.

"If you put a sack of stones
Under the banyan tree
The divine children
Will come down."

My three sons are Isac, Jacob
And Lastuan ("Last One")
Isac does all the talking
Gladys aged twelve
Does the translating
"You boys and girls
Are ropes of John Frum
You live together in a witty cabin
And the night is for dancing."

Tell the other people
These are my desires:
"Bathe together in the lake
Look calm
Heavy buying in the stores
Days of rest: Friday, Monday
Other days: recreation.

"My planes are coming
With prefab houses for all
With radios salaries
For teachers
Means of conveyance."

2

I Neloiag
Am John Frum King
I level the mountain
Where my planes will come
I am King of American Flyers
I can arrest the British
With my telegraph
Though they declare me insane.

I am the Instigator
Just one of the ropes
But Isac the Voice
Speaks to me direct
In secret bushes
Banning colors
On Thursdays only

(Red yellow and blue
Strictly forbidden
Since red is blood
Blue is sickness
Yellow is death.)

3

Isac commanded with a man's voice. "Pull the tickets." We
went together to the store. We moved the people out of our
way. We climbed over the counters. We carried out all the
instructions. Tore off the price tags ("tickets"). With tags
all gone the store was cleaner. And it had to be made
cleaner. A preparation. Now John Frum can come with his
army and Cargo.

(The action was defined by police as "The affair of the
tickets." "The defendants entered a European store at
White Sands, leapt over the counters and pulled the tickets
off the goods.")

I am only
One of the ropes
I communicate instructions
Isac is the one who commands
Sundown Thursday
With a man's voice
"Armies
Cargoes
Coming by jet-plane."

4

Then there appeared to be another uprising by these fanat-
ics. Those who had been exiled to Malekula sent a lot of

coconuts back to their home village. These were to be carefully planted on the site of their houses.

The Presbyterian Missionary (disturbed and looking for trouble) saw in this act a symbolic message. Others said this was very doubtful. The agent ordered the coconuts to be dug up. The natives said it was simply a matter of introducing a new variety of nut.

REPORT: "Police measures reasonably effective in spite of coconuts. Leaders however continue propagating ideas in new place of residence. Reunions held near (French) district office. No manifestations. Ropes of John Frum reported north of Port Sandwich and across Straits at Ambrym. Ropes bring message to Presbyterian village. Exiles not fully responsible for what happens after that. Village organized by native militia. Daily drill under capts and lieuts. Change trousers at each meeting. Former Presbyterian natives declare they have no further need of missionaries who can go home at earliest convenience. Boys resume contact with ancestor Volcano Deity by telephone. Woman sees light on crag and hears bell. Moonlight procession to crag with guitars and dancing. Sound of ancestor bell is heard (somewhat muffled and uncertain). They wait. As no further communication is forthcoming from Volcano voice, woman suggests slaughter of cats. This is done. People pay all debts in stores and throw remaining money into the sea.

Baimbai money belong me he come
Face belong you fella King
Take 'em, he go back!

5

And the white ship
Of the Messageries
Came as the voice said
Watchers day and night
Saw it appear
Newly painted white
Plenty of Cargo
Unloaded in the usual place.

"The Chief went to ask the missionary if he were really
sure the goods were for him."

6

Kumala O
We are yams
From Craig Cove to Ambrym
We are potatoes
All over the Islands
Kumala O

It is known that gold pounds were thrown into the sea at
Ranmuhu and Fanu and the bell of Likon rang in the bush
for the night meeting.
Then the missionary
Took his departure.

7

"The movement reached Paama, a wholly Presbyterian
island, where the natives began to rid themselves of all
money and to kill the pigs." It spread to Epi and Pente-
cost. Many visited the defendants at Port Sandwich. "The
exiles had great prestige."

8

Everything in the world has a cause and aim. So Jonfroom
mvt. has procedures of its own.

Two main rules: 1. People will stop going to Church
                 2. People will drink a lot of kava.
These rules are still strongly carried out at present.

9

Dear Father Somo,

    I am Joe. I forgot something I had to tell you I say
to you Somo and Sam Nako that I come here to Vila.
The government at Tanna tied you up but that is
nothing. Do not forget the tobacco which came to me
from John Frum and Nauka. John Frum wanted
Nauka to show him the road to come out. Nauka
did not know the road so he sent the tobacco to me,
to you Somo and to Sam Nako. I made the road so
that all the chiefs could go and shake hands with
John Frum because I was not there but Karaua soft-
ened his heart and showed the chiefs John Frum.
John Frum only spoke to them because he did not
see me with them. He asked Karaua where I was
and Karaua told him I was in Vila.

    John Frum and I were together and we arranged
that all the others should come to Vila. We talked
together about them (the chiefs) and we arranged
that the chiefs should follow us when they came out
of jail.

John Frum and I came to Sidni [mission village near Lenakel] to look for a place for a house. John Frum pointed where his house was to stand just alongside mine but he did not describe what kind of house. So listen well you Somo and Sam Nako; Nako will provide three men, Natoga will provide three men: Bangor will send three men to build the house and Sidni will provide the food for the workers. You are not to say that the house is for John Frum or for me but just say it is a company or a communal house.

We two are only waiting for the chiefs to go back to Tanna and when the house is ready you will send word to us and John Frum and I will come to the house you will have prepared at Sidni. Then John Frum will gather the white men and talk to them. He will send his son to America to bring the king. You must not be afraid. He showed me aeroplanes at Lonopina [name for Tukosmeru, the highest mountain in Tanna] as thick as the bush.

You two must conceal the contents of this letter. This is not my letter, John Frum is sitting by me as I write.

This is the end of my letter but John Frum's is underneath.

john the great
my brother here is joe: my name is karaperamun
every thing is near to me
see us two joe captain cockle shell.

I am joe. I am saying to you two brothers and father that this spirit writing speaks to you these four lines only which you see. See how his writing has not capital letters. He says cockle shell. The meaning of this is that we two fit like the two halves of a cockle shell. Everything will come from Sidni Jonfrum wants you to answer this letter by the Morinda.

IX. DIALOG WITH MISTER CLAPCOTT

Letter to Mr. Clapcott sir you sonofabitch you notice we
    have now cut down your coconut trees
You have messed with all our women and when this was
    pointed out you have not desisted
And now we are going to fix you Clapcott five men
Will come and you will not hear them come
Since you are deaf
You will be shot and parts will be cut off
Parts also eaten
Because of which
Our dead shall rise
Black shall be white
Cargo shall come to Santo
Ancestors come home in white ship
From where you sent them you sonofabitch
With all your papers.

We will unload the Cargo in our new store
Sharing it among all who have paid their dues.

We sing this nightletter against you Mr. Clapcott
    and tomorrow
All the bodies riding on the winds of resurrection
Shall have white skins because you are gone
So for you Mr. Clapcott we sing this message
Five special delivery bullets in the chest tomorrow
And then our ship will come from America
Where there is no more death

Repeat nightletter Mr. Clapcott sir you sonofabitch
    you notice
Ghost wind has blown down your coconut trees
And your beach is very red.

X. AND A FEW MORE CARGO SONGS

1. When Sir Harry asked Government Agent Nicol "who that woman" was the Agent took her by the hair, pulled her head back and opened her mouth inspecting her teeth and replied: "Oh, that's Rosie."

2. John the Broom is a big man with shining buttons
He is hidden from women
(Except Gladys a little girl)
He will provide the money.

3. Nicol came with twenty police and tied John Frum
    to a tree
But everyone said it was not the real John Frum
For John the True
Had gone to America
To confer with Rusefel
To get a Black American Army
And Liberator Planes
All flown by Blacks
And full of dollars
To let out every man
In Nicol's prison.

4. *Players Cigarettes:*
A prophetic interpretation
Of the ikon.

"Jake Navy he is player and smoker
Good fella seen in vision
By the faithful
Lives in a beard and a battleship lifebelt
He will send his delegate
(Noah's avatar)
To take the place
Of Agent Nicol"
Is everybody happy?

5. Ghost wind come O Brother
Sell me the shivering
For a little piece of paper
Sell me the shivering
For a little piece of Whiteman Times
To roll my cigarette
To blow my Whiteman smoke
In Ghostwind good feeling
O sell me the shivering brother
Give me a ticket to the happy dark
Trade me a houseful of rifles
For a new white skin
In Dark Ghost Wind
Sell me the shivering, Brother,
For Whiteman good times!

WEST

I. DAY SIX O'HARE TELEPHANE

Comes a big slow fish with tailfins erect in light smog
And one other leaves earth
Go trains of insect machines
Thirtynine generals signal eight
Contact barrier four

A United leaves earth
Square silver bug moves into shade under wing building
Standby train three black bugs indifferent
A week after he got sick
A long beetle called Shell
On a firm United basis
Long heavy-assed American dolphin touches earth
Please come to the counter
Where we have your camera
Eastern Airlines has your camera
And two others drink coffee
Out of yellow paper cups

Big Salvador not cooled off yet
From sky silver but
Hotel Fenway takes off at once
To become Charles' Wain

"The wise man who has acquired mental vacuity is not
concerned with contemplation or its absence"

Forty stories of window seats available
Watcher stands on turntable ensemble
Counts passing generals
In curtains and spaces leaving earth
Two bugs like trucks
With airplane's noses
Ride our fables
Armored with earmuffs
Racing alone across asphalt sound
Armored against desert
All members
Not numbered yet

All clear neons come to the confession
The racing numbers
Are not remembered

Big Panam leaves earth
Gets Tax Man started into death
I'll get the teachers expanded
Turn your hat
Over your breath
Small dapper North Central is green for woods
And arrives safe
Flight information requires Queen
All green Braniff leaves earth for Pole
And big United Doppelganger slides very close
Seeking the armed savers

It points at us all and it is named:
"PHILIP."

It swings. Body No. 7204 U
In case of mountain death
Discovers Teacher Jackson
Wins Colorado team maybe
In the snow
In the rare acts

Check tables for Vance Cooper
Advance with boarding arts
The glide area has now won and
Boy you got a lotta SPREAD

Hello say the mignonnes
You can go to bed
You can go to the gorgeous
Community period and

"Though appearing to act he does not engage in action."

Muffled the vice of Lou'ville smoke
The front
Hello money got to go pump earnings
Into bug MM2 for Derby Dad
Telling arrival is a copperhead
Big Mafia sits with mainlining blonde
Regular Bounder Marlo
Come meet world muffin at ticket counter
Ticket country
Mr. Kelsey
Mr. Kelsey
You are now wanted
In ticket country

"It is not distant and it is not the object of attainment."

Come we will pump our money into dogs
And lift our gorgeous raids sky high
Over the sunlit periods
Bending aluminum angels and Tax Man
And giddy grey girls
Over the suburban highschools
Our glide has won
Our teacher has dropped out
Our giant vocal captains are taking off
Whooping and plunging like world police
On distant outside funnels
Stainless diagrams sink
Into muddy air
We leave earth and act
Going to San
Patterns slide down we go for clear
Sanitation heaven
Combing the murky
Surface of profit
San Franciscan wing over abstract
Whorls wide sandpits watershapes
Forms and prints and grids

Invent a name for a town
Any town
"Sewage Town."
And day six is a climbing sun
A day of memory.

"Having finally recognized that the Self is Brahman and
that existence and non-existence are imagined, what should
such a one, free of desires, know, say or do?"

Should he look out of the windows
Seeking Self-Town?
Should the dance of Shivashapes
All over flooded prairies
Make hosts of (soon) Christ-Wheat
Self-bread which could also be
Squares of Buddha-Rice
Or Square Maize about those pyramids
Same green
Same brown, same square
Same is the Ziggurat of everywhere
I am one same burned Indian
Purple of my rivers is the same shed blood
All is flooded
All is my Vietnam charred
Charred by my co-stars
The flying generals.

"He who sees reality in the universe may try to negate it."

To deny linoleum badges
Deride the false tile field floor
Of the great Illinois bathroom
Lettered all over
With busy-signals

To view the many branches of the Shiva-cakes
The veined paddies or pastries
The burned trays of the Ming prairie
Or the porcelain edges
Of the giant Mother Mississippi

"His actions in this world are appearances only."

Appearances of a city
And disappearances
Dubuque dragging its handkerchiefs
Into a lake of cirrus
(Gap with one long leg of extended highway)
Compasses
Veiled
Valed
Vale!

"Not seeing, he appears to see."

A lake of cottons
Iowa needs names

High above this milk
There is a race-leader or power passenger
At odds with the white rest
The cloud captains
An individual safe
A strong-box enclosed self
A much more jealous reason
One among many
Who will have his way
A logical black provider
For only one family
Flying with a fortune in stamps
He stands in line with the others
Outside the highest toilet in the world
To establish a record in rights
High above the torment
Of milling wind and storms

124

We are All High Police Thors
Holding our own weapons
Into the milk mist each alone
As our battering ram
Fires us all into Franciscan West
As strangers in the same line
United in indifferent skies
Where nobody needs any anger.

Not seeing he is thought to be over Sioux Falls
Getting hungry
Not seeing he is thought to see
Saying "It is there"
The family combination shelter and fun
Room where all is possible.

Sinbad returning from the vines of wire
Makes his savage muffled voice
With playboy accents
To entertain the momentary mignonnes
As if he meant it all in fun

Sinbad returning from Arab voices
With his own best news for everybody boy
Says: "Wellfed cities
Are all below
Standing in line
Beneath enormous gas
Waiting to catch our baseball."

Sinbad the voyager makes his muscles of utterance
Soundless lips entertain the merveilles

Merveilles les vignes
De fil de fer
Hongrie
Les vagues barbares de l'est
Get ready for your invasion baby
Dr. Farges awaits you with his syringe
And Tom Swift rides by below
On his invisible mammoth mountains of art
The granite sides of Rushmore
Now showing four Walt Whitmans
Who once entrusted the nation to rafts

    Four secret presidents
    With stone ideas
    Who mumble under gas
    Our only government
    Has provided free and says:
    "This mildly toxic invention can harm none
    But the enemy."

Merveilles! Secrets! Deadly plans for distant places!
And all high males are flying far west
In a unanimous supermarket of beliefs
Seeking one only motto
For "L'imagination heureuse":
WHY NOT TRY EVERYTHING?

II. AT THIS PRECISE MOMENT OF HISTORY

1. At this precise moment of history
    With Goody-two-shoes running for Congress
    We are testing supersonic engines
    To keep God safe in the cherry tree.
    When I said so in this space last Thursday
    I meant what I said: power struggles.

2. You would never dream of such corn. The colonials in
    sandalwood like running wide open and available for
    protection. You can throw them away without a refund.

3. Dr. Hanfstaengel who was not called Putzi except by
    those who did not know him is taped in the national
    archives. J. Edgar Hoover he ought to know
    And *does* know.

    But calls Dr. Hanfstaengel Putzi nevertheless
    Somewhere on tape in the
    Archives.

    He (Dr. H.) is not a silly man.
    He left in disgust
    About the same time Shirley Temple
    Sat on Roosevelt's knee
    An accomplished pianist
    A remembered personality
    He (Dr. H.) began to teach
    Immortal anecdotes

To his mother a Queen Bee
In the American colony.

4. What is your attitude toward historical subjects?
   —Perhaps it's their size!

5. When I said this in space you would never believe
   Corn Colonel was so expatriated.
   —If you think you know,
   Take this wheel
   And become standard.

6. She is my only living mother
   This bee of the bloody arts
   Bandaging victims of Saturday's dance
   Like a veritable sphinx
   In a totally new combination.

7. The Queen Mother is an enduring vignette
       at an early age.
   Now she ought to be kept in submersible
       decompression chambers

   For a while.

8. What is your attitude toward historical subjects
   Like Queen Colonies?
   —They are permanently fortified
   For shape retention.

9. Solid shades
   Seven zippered pockets
   Close to my old place

Waiting by the road
Big disk brakes
Spinoff
Zoom
Long lights stabbing at the
Two together piggyback
In a stark sports roadster

Regretting his previous outburst
Al loads his Cadillac
With lovenests.

10. She is my only living investment
    She examines the housing industry
    Counts 3.5 million postwar children
    Turning twenty-one
    And draws her own conclusion
    In the commercial fishing field.

11. Voice of little sexy ventriloquist mignonne:
    "Well I think all of us are agreed and sincerely I my-
    self believe that honest people on both sides have got
    it all on tape. Governor Reagan thinks that nuclear
    wampums are a last resort that ought not to be re-
    sorted." (But little mignonne went right to the point
    with: "We have a commitment to fulfill and we better
    do it quick." No dupe she!)

All historians die of the same events at least twice.

13. I feel that I ought to open this case with an apology.
    Dr. H. certainly has a beautiful voice. He is not a silly
    man. He is misunderstood even by Presidents.

14. You people are criticizing the Church but what are you going to put in her place? Sometime sit down with a pencil and paper and ask yourself what you've got that the Church hasn't.

15. Nothing to add
    But the big voice of a detective
    Using the wrong first names
    In national archives.

16. She sat in shocking pink with an industrial zipper specially designed for sitting on the knees of presidents in broad daylight. She spoke the president's mind. "We have a last resort to be resorted and we better do it quick." He wondered at what he had just said.

17. It was all like running wideopen in a loose gown
    Without slippers
    At least someplace.

III. GHOST DANCE: Prologue

AMERICAN HORSE FAST THUNDER SPOTTED
HORSE PRETTY BACK GOOD LANCE PRESENT
NOV 27 1890

We were made many promises by the Commissioners but
we never heard from them since.
They talked nice to us and after we signed they took our
land cut down our rations.
They made us believe we would get full sacks if we signed
but instead our sacks are empty.
Our chickens were all stolen our cattle were killed our
crops were entirely lost because we were absent talking
with the Commission.
We are told if we do as white men do we will be better off
but we are getting worse off every year.

When we were in Washington the President
The Secretary the Commissioner promised
We would get back a million lbs. of beef
Taken from us and the Bill
Passed Congress
But the Commissioner
Refused
To give us
Any meat.

IV. GHOST DANCE

1. ALL THE OLD TIME PROPHECIES ABOUT THE WHITES COMING TO THIS COUNTRY AND ABOUT GUNS HAVE COME TRUE SO WHAT WE HAVE DREAMED ABOUT THE END IS PROBABLY TRUE AS WELL.

2. Dr. Sam said Wodziwob was the real Starter. Four Paiute men from Surprise went to hear him. He was around Reno. Four Paiute men went from Surprise to Reno to hear the Starter. Was he telling the Truth?

3. Wodziwob said: "There are a lot of people telling the news but they are not telling it right. What I said was: 'A train is coming' and my real dream was about that train. People made it out different. What Wodziwob said was correct. It was then 1869 and a train was on its way to Hollywood.
What Dr. Sam said was also correct. Wodziwob was the Starter.

4. Wodziwob first gave out news the dead were coming. They were all coming with cups in their hands to drink from. When would they arrive? In about four years.

5. It was announced that the dead were not coming by train.

6. Zonchen reported that he had seen the dead coming. They were on their way. I saw Zonchen when he was down in Reno fifty years ago. I don't know whether he was just a chief or whether he dreamed these things himself.

7. The Starter said the dead were on their way with the Supreme Ruler. They were all coming in a group. No distinction would exist any more between races.

8. He preached at Pyramid Lake: "Our Fathers are coming. Our Mothers are coming. Dance without stopping. Every morning, swim, wash, paint. Paint yourselves black, white, red. Don't stop dancing. Be always happy."

9. They danced five nights without bells, a fire in the center. There was no preaching against the whites. The songs were all new brought by dreamers from the Land of the Dead. Many dancers fainted.

10. Minnie Jo said: "There were Washo doctors who spoke with the dead before the Paiute miracle men and they still do. Our doctors were always talking with the dead. If they say the dead will return, we believe them."

11. The State Capitol Building at Carson City was finished but there was not yet a fence around it. Weneyuga came to the Washo and said he was Dr. Frank. He gave dances and said dead relatives were about to return from the South. "As the dead draw near, put your hands in front of your faces and spread the fingers. Look through the fingers and you will recognize your own relatives."

12. Dr. Frank said that when the dead returned all the white people would disappear and halfbreed children would drop dead. There would be no more race conflict.

13. Dr. Frank said that if he dipped his hands in a stream and roiled the water, the water would then become poison-

ous to white people. But he added that he never did this. He also made red pigment form on the stones of the State Capitol Building. He used this pigment on converts.

14. He had a staff with red and white rings around it and an eagle feather on top. He planted it by his head when he lay down to sleep. He did not tell what it was for but he believed in it. Sometimes where he planted the stick in the ground he would dig up gold watches military buttons silver chains and insignia.

15. A very serious dance was held at Reno. It lasted five nights. There were no fun steps. Children had trances. Dr. Frank rubbed his body with phosphorous from old Chinese matches to make it shine in the dark. The song he dreamed and sang this time was: "Indian Father sitting place sound of the wind."

16. He drew a line on the ground. Everybody who stepped over the line would meet a dead relative.

17. The Washo doctors said Dr. Frank was an imposter. He headed north with one disciple.

18. Dr. George gave this rule: "Whenever you dream, paint your face red and white and do what your dream tells you. Otherwise you will turn to stone."

19. Dr. George came to the mouth of Lost River where he found Captain Jack and the people. He came in winter when no grass was growing. He said that when the grass was eight inches high the dead would return. The deer and

all the animals would return. "The whites will burn up and vanish without leaving any ashes. Dance or you will be turned to stone."

20. Then everybody danced and jumped in the river. They came out of the water with ice in their hair. They told what the coming-back-people wanted us to do.

21. Dr. George stretched a rope around the dance ground and said: "Anyone who tries to molest me will turn to stone as soon as he steps over the rope." The Superintendent came and stepped over the rope. He did not turn to stone. He arrested Dr. George for making the people crazy.

22. Bogus Tom wanted to take the songs about the dead to Oregon but the white people said anyone who sang or danced in Oregon would go to jail. Bogus Tom then showed them papers he had got from a lawyer in Oregon and they allowed him to give a dance. But it was just like church. No drunken people were allowed in.

23. *Cornwallis* (Oregon) *Gazette,* Jan. 4, 1873: "Scarcely an Indian on the Siletz Agency does not express perfect confidence in the prophecies. They are gathering upon the reservations. They are nightly engaged in war dances and decorating themselves with paint and feathers. They are governed by messengers and spies from other tribes. Whites were warned of this last summer by friendly squaws who said the dead would come to life, war would be waged on whites, Indians would take possession of their former hunting grounds and peaceful homes."

24. The Superintendent of the Siletz Reservation denied that the dancing had a warlike character. He said: "I presume two thirds of those who engaged in these dances did so for mere amusement." He was not believed. He said the dances were "less harmful than gambling." The white people did not agree.

25. Old Chocolate Hat was head dreamer for Captain Dick. He stayed with us until he died just lately. He used to shake all over when he told of those days.

26. Baptiste was coming home from the Warm House Dance. He saw a black and white hound run under his house. Then he saw his daughter who had been dead for years go into his house. He was happy because the dead had now started to return. He planned what he would say when he went into his house and found his daughter sitting there alive. When he went in he looked all around and found no one.

27. John Watchino said he would not go to Bogus Tom's Warm House Dance. He added that the dead relatives were not coming back either. He said: "Our God gave us the Indian religion and there was nothing in it about Warm House. Our old religion said the world would change but it never said we would live to see it."

28. Dr. Charlie was asked to get in a trance and find out if the dead were really on the way. Dr. Charlie said his spirit person, Meadowlark, met not one dead person coming from spirit land. This news shook the faith of many dancers.

29. Bogus Tom said: "You dance this. It is a good word. It is like church."

30. Annie Peterson said Coquille Charlie carried the dance around only to make money. He did not say the dead would return or tell what would happen to the whites. Nobody had any visions at Charlie's dance.

31. After a while the dreaming stopped and the Dream Dance turned into a Feather Dance. It was just a fun dance. It was mostly a white man's show.

NOTES ON SOURCES

Publisher's Note: Before he left Our Lady of Gethsemani Monastery in Kentucky in the summer of 1968, setting out on the first stages of the Asian journey from which he did not return, Thomas Merton sent me the typescript of this first book of *The Geography of Lograire*. In his letters he said he hoped to extend the poem, that he envisaged it as a "work in progress" of considerable length, but that this first section could stand by itself and was ready for publication except for proof corrections.

In preparing the typescript for the printer, Barbara Harr, Associate Editor at New Directions, and I made few changes. The inconsistent punctuation was altered only in a few lines where necessary for clarity (once Merton had chided me for wanting to put periods at the end of every stanza in an earlier book) and only obvious misspellings were corrected. It was possible to correct a half dozen small typing errors by checking back to an earlier typed version, which probably dates from Spring, 1968, and to the holograph notebook in which the greater part of the poem appears first to have been composed. This notebook is now a part of the archive at The Thomas Merton Room of Bellarmine-Ursuline College Library, Louisville. It runs to about 160 written pages. The first page is inscribed: "THE NEWSNATCH INVENTION by Thomas Merton 1967," with an epigraph from Gaston Bachelard below: "Rendre imprévisible la parole n'est-il pas un apprentissage de la liberté?" However, I am not certain whether "The Newsnatch Invention" was Merton's first choice of title for *The Geography of Lograire* because the first eleven pages of the notebook contain drafts of short poems that were not incorporated in *Lograire*. A draft of the present prologue begins on the twelfth page of the notebook. From that point onward most of the pages have notes, or quotations from his reading, or drafts that found their way into the final version. There is fairly drastic revision of phrasing between the lines in the notebook and those in the first typescript as well as many additions of amplifying details and even new ideas. "The Geography of Lograire" is written at the head of the twenty-third page above the first draft of the section now called "Queens Tunnel." Sister M. Thérèse, a friend of the poet, has kindly supplied a note which explains the genesis of the name "Lograire."

In the Author's Note (page 1) which accompanied the final typescript Merton tells how he drew on his reading for material: "In this wide-angle mosaic of poems and dreams I have without scruple mixed what is my own experience with what is almost everybody else's. . . . what is given [from other books] is most often literal and accurate quotation with slight editing and with of course much personal arrangement. And where more drastic editing is called for by my own dream, well, I have dreamed it." Merton had prepared a few footnotes, acknowledging his sources, and had he lived, would have supplied source credits for the others on his proofs. With help from Brother Patrick and Father Augustine of Gethsemani, the staff of Bellarmine-Ursuline College Library, and the Trustees of the Merton Legacy Trust, Miss Harr and I have provided source notes wherever we have been able to identify sources, either through recollections about the poet's reading or from his references in the notebook. I hope that readers able to identify still-unlisted sources will send them to me so that they may be included in later editions. Meanwhile I beg indulgence of authors and copyright owners of works from which passages or ideas may have been taken that are not yet specifically acknowledged.   —J. LAUGHLIN

In reply to the Publisher's question as to whether from notes or conversations with Thomas Merton, I might be able to identify the name "Lograire," I recall that when he read me portions of the poem, then in progress, I asked him about the origin of the title, as I suspected it might have a connection with some mythical country in Arthurian Romance. He then explained that the real name of the French lyric poet, François Villon, was François *Des Loges,* and it was from this surname (really the name of a place) that he had "created" his own country of "Lograire" and that "loges" referred to little huts or cabins used by woodcutters or foresters. There is an immediate relevance not only to Merton's having been at one time chief forester of his Trappist community, with his lookout post in a tower on the highest hill, but perhaps more importantly to his own hermitage on a wooded rise near the Monastery of Gethsemani. The term "Des Loges" has certain interesting historical significances as well that seem pertinent. According to the *Grand Encyclopédie Larousse* it refers to a "pelouse" in the middle of the forest of Saint Germain, before the *Maison des Loges,* a monastery and royal residence destroyed during the Hundred Years War, that had replaced the original cabins or "loges." In 1644, Anne of Austria built a new monastery there which became a place of pilgrimage and of the "Fêtes des Loges."

SISTER M. THÉRÈSE LENTFOEHR

SOURCES

Page

19 *Thonga Lament.* Based on *The Life of A South African Tribe* by Henri Junod, London, 1927, II, p. 423.

20 *Hare's Message.* Based on *The Khoisan People of South Africa: Bushmen and Hottentots,* London, 1930, pp. 357-8.

21 *A Clever Stratagem.* Based on a passage in *The Soul of the Bantu* by W. C. Willoughby, Doubleday, Doran & Com-

pany, Inc., Garden City, 1928, page 135. (Copyright 1928 by Doubleday, Doran & Company, Inc.)

24 *Ce Xochitl.* Fray Bernardino de Sahagun (1499-1590) wrote the *Historia general de las cosas de Nueva España.* The lines on the Mayan festival honoring the god Xochilhuitl appear to have been taken from this work, especially from Book 4, Chapter 7. Merton seems not to have followed closely either the translation by Charles E. Dibble and Arthur J. O. Anderson (*General History of the Things of New Spain,* published by The School of American Research and The University of Utah, Monographs of the School of American Research and Museum of New Mexico, Santa Fe, No. 14, 1957) or the version of Fanny R. Bandelier (*A History of Ancient Mexico,* Fisk University Press, Nashville, 1932); Merton may have made his own translation from the Spanish or he may have used yet another English text.

26 Bishop Diego de Landa (1524-1579) wrote the *Relación de las cosas de Yucatan.* Merton probably used the translation by A. M. Tozzer, Papers of the Peabody Museum, Harvard, Volume XVIII, Cambridge, 1941. He may also have consulted the Spanish edition, with introduction and notes by Hector Perez Martinez, published by Editorial Pedro Robredo, Mexico, D. F., 1938. (Bishop Landa is also noted for having burned as many books of "heathen idolatry and diabolical superstition" as he could find; these were the priceless authoritative texts of the ancient Mayan holy writings, probably including some writings related to the *Chilam Balam* books which Merton quotes in succeeding passages.)

27 *The Ladies of Tlatilco.* The references to early Mexican art are from *Indian Art of Mexico and Central America*

by Miguel Covarrubias. (© Alfred A. Knopf, Inc., 1957)
The Covarrubias book contains illustrations of animal-
shaped vessels and of a two-headed figurine. The text, espe-
cially on pages 13 through 27, discusses the pottery, food
and agricultural products, scant clothing and hair-bleaching
processes of the people of Tlatilco, as well as the possible
relation of their pottery to Picasso's work and to the idea
of twins. The quotation concerning the vessel with the
funnel-shaped tail and gurgling ears is from Covarrubias,
page 21. The lines satirizing contemporary American ad-
vertisements might have been inspired by those in *The
New Yorker.*

31   *Chilam Balam* and *Dzules.* Stanza 10 of *Dzules* is taken
34   from *The Book of the Jaguar Priest: a Translation of the
Book of Chilam Balam of Tizimin,* with commentary by
Maud Worcester Makemson, Henry Schuman, New York,
1951. (Copyright 1951 by Henry Schuman, Inc.) Other
portions (though not all) of these two sections may also
have been derived from the Makemson book. Other pos-
sible sources for the Yucatan sections include Ralph L.
Roys, *The Book of Chilam Balam of Chumayel,* published
by the Carnegie Institution of Washington, 1933, as Publi-
cation No. 438; Ralph L. Roys, "The Maya Katun Proph-
ecies of the Books of Chilam Balam, Series I," in *Con-
tributions to American Anthropology and History,* Vol.
XII, No. 57, 1954, published by the Carnegie Institution of
Washington as Publication 606, 1960. Also, three articles
in *Contributions to American Anthropology and History,*
Vol. X, published by the Carnegie Institution of Washing-
ton, 1949: "The Maya Chronicles," translated by Alfredo
Barrera Vásquez and Sylvanus Griswold Morley, No. 48;
"Guide to the Codex Perez," by Ralph L. Roys, No. 49;
and "The Prophecies for the Maya Tuns or Years in the

Books of Chilam Balam of Tizimin and Mani," by Ralph
L. Roys, No. 51. Also: *The Ancient Maya,* by Sylvanus
Griswold Morley, 3rd ed., revised by George W. Brainerd,
Stanford University Press, 1956. Merton's notebook con-
tains many details noted from the Morley volume.

34 *Dzules.* Stanza 11 is taken from *El libro de los libros de
Chilam Balam,* translated (into Spanish) by Alfredo
Barrera Vásquez and Silvia Rendón, published by Fondo
de Cultura Económica, Mexico and Buenos Aires, 1st
edition, 1948, page 103. Other quotations in Spanish in
this section may also be from this source.

61 "There is a grain of sand in Lambeth which Satan cannot
find." William Blake: *Jerusalem,* II, 41, 15.

63 *The Ranters and Their Pleads.* The Ranters were a fanati-
cal sect in England in the 17th century. They were anti-
nomian, spiritualistic and pantheistic, believing that God
is in every creature. They attacked the established church,
the Bible, and the clergy, calling on people to listen only
to the voice of Christ within them. The unrest which they
generated, especially among the poor, led to accusations
of sexual license and to the suppression of the sect. Mer-
ton's source is Norman Cohn, *The Pursuit of the Millen-
nium,* Oxford University Press, New York, 1957. On pages
315-372, Cohn quotes at length from a number of seven-
teenth-century documents: writings of the Ranters, anti-
Ranter tracts, reports of the arrest of Ranters and statements
by Parliamentary acts and committees concerning them.
1. *The Routing of the Ranters.* An anti-Ranter tract, see
Cohn, p. 328. The quoted paragraph, from court hearings,
concerns a formerly-respectable matron allegedly corrupted
by the Ranters.
2. Merton has condensed and rephrased material from

Cohn, p. 329, concerning eight Ranters arrested in London on November 1, 1650. Primary sources quoted by Cohn include: *The Arraignment & Tryall with a Declaration of the Ranters* . . . , 1650; *Strange News From the Old-bayly or The Proofs, Examinations, Declarations, Indictments and Convictions of the Ranters, at the Sessions of Gaole-Delivery, held in the Old Bayly, the 18, 19, and 20 of this instant January* . . . , *1651;* and *The Ranters Ranting: with The apprehending, examinations, and confession* . . . , 1650.

3. Selected and condensed from Cohn, pp. 319-320, 330. Primary sources include: Thomas Edwards, "Gangraena, or a Catalogue and Discovery of Many of the Errours, Heresies, Blasphemies and pernicious Practices of the Sectaries of this time, vented and acted in England in these four last years," 1646, pp. 21 sq.; Edward Hyde, D.D., "A Wonder and yet no Wonder: a great Red Dragon in Heaven," 1651, pp. 24, 35 sq.; and Richard Baxter, "Reliquiae Baxterianae," 1696, pp. 76-77.

4. Slightly edited quotations from a Ranter named Clarkson, see Cohn, p. 330.

5. From the title of a tract by Humphrey Ellis: *Pseudochristus; Or, A true and faithful Relation of the Grand Impostures, Horrid Blasphemies, Abominable Practices, Gross Deceits; Lately spread abroad and acted in the County of Southampton* . . . , 1650. See Cohn, p. 330.

6. The first three phrases are excerpted from an Act of Parliament of 9th August, 1650, for the "Punishment of Atheistical, Blasphemous and Execrable Opinions." Quoted by H. Scobell in *A Collection of Acts and Ordinances* . . . , 1658, Part II, pp. 124-126; quoted again in Cohn, p. 325. The last paragraph is quoted from Cohn, p. 334. The primary source is an anti-Ranter tract entitled *The Ranters Religion or A faithfull and infallible Narrative of their*

damnable and diabolical opinions, with their detestable lives and actions. With a true discovery of some of their late prodigious pranks, and unparalleled deportments . . . , 1650. Title of tract quoted by Cohn, p. 328.

7. First paragraph rephrased from Cohn, pp. 335 ff. Other material quoted from a Ranter named Jacob Bauthemly (or Bauthumley, or Bottomley), condensed from Cohn, pp. 336-340.

8. First five phrases from titles of previously-noted tracts: *Strange News . . . , Arraignment and Tryall . . . ,* and *The Ranters Religion. . . .* See Cohn, pp. 328-329. Other material from Cohn, p. 323; the primary source is John Holland, "Smoke of the Bottomlesse Pit or, A More true and fuller Discovery of the Doctrine of those men which call themselves Ranters: or, The Mad Crew," 1651. The closing two lines of this stanza are from the titles of tracts previously noted.

9. From the stated aim of a Parliamentary committee, appointed June 14, 1650, to consider this problem. See Cohn, p. 325.

10. From the primary source by John Holland. See Cohn, p. 324.

69 *Kane Relief Expedition.* This section is based on Dr. James Laws' Journal of the Kane Relief Expedition, 1855, in the Stefansson Collection at Dartmouth College Library.

82 *East with Ibn Battuta.* Ibn Battuta (1304-1369), a Muslim from Morocco, left a colorful record of his *Travels in Asia and Africa, 1325-1354.* In this section Merton worked from the translation by H. A. R. Gibb, The Broadway Travellers Series, Routledge & Kegan Paul Ltd., London, 1929. "Love of the Sultan" (pp. 277-8); "Cairo 1326" (pp. 51-3); "Syria" (page 61: "The Ten Companions": "the most prominent members of Muhammad's entourage . . . greatly

revered by the orthodox [Sunnites]; the Shi'ites on the other hand, regard them much as Judas Iscariot is regarded in the Christian tradition. Their especial hatred is reserved for Omar, who was responsible for the election of the first Caliph and was himself the second, and whom they blame accordingly for the exclusion of Ali from the succession to which he was designated . . . by the Prophet." Gibb's note.); "The Nusayris" (pp. 62-3. "the Mahdi": the last iman, or leader of the faithful, whose appearance is awaited by the Sunnites.); "Mecca" (direct quotation from page 76); "Delhi" (page 226); "Calicut" (pp. 235 & 240-2). (An edition of *The Travels of Ibn Battuta,* edited by Gibb, is also published in this country by Cambridge University Press, two volumes, 1958 and 1962.)

89 *East with Malinowski.* This section is loosely based on Bronislaw Malinowski's South Sea Island journal, *A Diary in the Strict Sense of the Term,* published by Harcourt, Brace & World in 1967. (Copyright © 1967 by A. Valetta Malinowska) Merton, however, has done extensive rephrasing, condensation, and rearrangement.

91 *Cargo Songs.* Merton was deeply interested in the Cargo cults of Melanesia and read extensively on the subject. He taped a long lecture-essay on "Cargo Theology" which has not yet been published, basing his factual material principally on three books: *Mambu, A Melanesian Millennium* by K. O. L. Burridge, Methuen & Co., Ltd., London, 1960 (© Kenelm Burridge 1960); *Road Belong Cargo, A Study of the Cargo Movement in the Southern Madang District, New Guinea* by Peter Lawrence, Melbourne University Press & Manchester University Press, Manchester, 1964 (© 1964 Peter Lawrence); and *The Trumpet Shall Sound, A Study of "Cargo" Cults in Melanesia* by Peter Worsley, second, augmented edition, MacGibbon & Kee,

London & Schocken Books, New York, 1968 (Copyright © 1968 by Peter Worsley). In a letter to Naomi Burton Stone, dated February 27, 1968, Merton explained some of the special significance which the Cargo myths had for him:

"Cargo movements properly so called originated in New Guinea and Melanesia around the end of the 19th century and developed there especially after World War II. But analogous movements have been cropping up everywhere in formerly colonial countries, and starting from Cargo as such I tend to find analogies all over the place, not only in Black Power but even to some extent in Catholic renewal as practised by some types.

"A Cargo movement is a messianic or apocalyptic cult movement which confronts a crisis of cultural change by certain magic and religious ways of acting out what seems to be the situation and trying to get with it, controlling the course of change in one's own favor (group) or in the line of some interpretation of how things ought to be. In some sense Marxism is a kind of Cargo cult. But strictly speaking, Cargo cults are means by which primitive and underprivileged people believe they can obtain manufactured goods by an appeal to supernatural powers (ancestors, spirits, etc.) and by following a certain constant type of pattern which involves: a) a complete rejection and destruction of the old culture with its goods and values b) adoption of a new attitude and hope of immediate Cargo, as a result of and reward for the rejection of the old. This always centers around some prophetic personage who brings the word, tells what is to be done, and organizes the movement.

"Though all this may seem naive and absurd to western 'civilized' people, I, in common with some of the anthropologists, try to spell out a deeper meaning. Cargo is relevant to everyone in a way. It is a way in which primitive people not only attempt by magic to obtain the goods they feel to be unjustly denied them, but also and more importantly a way of spelling out their conception of the injustice, their sense that basic human relationships are being ignored, and their hope of restoring the right order of things. If they want Cargo it is not only because they need material things but because Cargo will establish them as equal to the white man and give them an identity as respectable as his. But if they believe in Cargo it is because they believe in their own fundamental human worth and believe it can be shown in this way."

1. Sir William MacGregor. From Worsley, quoting Murray (page 51).
2. "The anthropologist lay low." Based on Malinowski's *Diary in the Strict Sense of the Term,* pages 199-202. Stanzas 5, 11, 17, 19, and 20 in this section are also based on Malinowski; Malinowski's illnesses, his reading, his reminiscences of friends and of his mother, the islander Igua, and other relevant topics are mentioned recurrently in the *Diary.* Merton, however, has done a great deal of rephrasing and rearrangement.
3. "Meanwhile four natives must hang." Worsley (page 51).
Stanzas 6-10. Worsley (pp. 52-3).
12. *"Ein ganz eigentümlich Vorgang."* ("A very peculiar event.") Worsley, quoting Wilhelm van Baar (page 108, n.) "Blackfela Catholic Mambu." Worsley (pp. 106-7).
13. *"Ein undankbares, schweres Missionsfeld."* ("A thankless, hard field for missionaries.") Worsley, quoting Höltker (page 107).
Stanzas 15, 16 and 18. Worsley (pp. 110-13).

96 *Place Names.* The chronology of European contacts in the Southern Madang District is based on Lawrence (pp. 34-7).

98 *Tibud Maclay.* Based on Lawrence (pp. 61-7). "Tibud": a god. "Djamans": Germans.

100 *Sewende (Seven Day).* 1. This section was suggested by an incident reported by Burridge (pp. 9-10). "Sewende": Pidgin for Seventh Day Adventist. "Big Belong": from *"bigpela bolong ol gat ap"* (God). 2. Based on Burridge (pp. 2-3). 3. Kaum. (Kaumaibu). A Kanaka Cargo prophet who led the Bagasin Rebellion of 1944 and was imprisoned by the Australian authorities. Kaum is treated in some depth by Lawrence (see the index to *Road Belong Cargo*) who tells of him: "He told [his followers] that while he had been in prison he had died as result of severe treatment by the native police. He had then gone to Heaven and seen God-Kilibob, who had given him a new skin—it would turn white in due course—a new name, Konsel (Councillor), and instructions to perform new ritual, which would bring ships and aircraft with cargo to Madang. . . . When the cargo arrived, God-Kilibob would cause an earthquake and tidal wave to destroy the Europeans." (page 163).

102 *Cargo Catechism.* Paragraphs 1-4 of this section are based on Lawrence's account of the "Third Cargo Belief" (pp. 15 *et seq.*). "Anut": God in the Madang area vernacular. In this myth, which the New Guineans invented from teachings of the missionaries, God punishes Ham (the ancestor of black people) for seeing his father Noah naked by taking away his "Cargo" (manufactured goods), which is then given only to his brothers, Shem and Japheth (the white man). "Heraus": New Guinea was first a German

colony; *"rausim"*: Pidgin for "root out." Paragraphs 5-10 are freely derived from the accounts in Lawrence and Burridge of the Cargo Cult leaders Manu and Yali.

105 *John the Volcano.* This entire section is either quoted or adapted, with imaginative additions, from an article by Jean Guiart, "The John Frum Movement in Tanna [New Hebrides]," in *Oceania,* published in Sydney by the Australian National Research Council, Volume XXII, Number 3, March, 1952. The letter in Stanza 9 is quoted verbatim from Guiart's appendix, where it has the heading: "Translation of Letter from Private Joe Nalpin to his Father Somo and to Sam Nako, Chief at Lenakel, Tanna." John Frum is also treated at length in Worsley (pp. 152-60).

113 *Dialog with Mister Clapcott.* See Worsley (pp. 148-9). A British planter, Clapcott, was murdered in 1923 at Tasmalum on the island of Espiritu Santo (New Hebrides) by the followers of a cult leader named Runovoro. He had promised that if the natives killed the Europeans, the dead would arise, and ancestors would return from a distant place where the whites had sent them, coming in a great white ship loaded with Cargo—for distribution to paid-up members of his movement.

115 *And a Few More Cargo Songs.* 1. From Worsley (page 152 n.), quoting Sir Harry Luke, *From a South Seas Diary.* 2 & 3. Mostly from Worsley (pp. 153-7) with perhaps some touches from Guiart.

119 *Day Six O'Hare Telephane.* The interpolated passages are from a relatively unknown Vedanta work, *Ashtavakra Gita,* translated by Hari Prasad Shastri and published by Shanti Sadan, London. Specifically quoted are: "The wise man who . . ." Chapter 17, verse 18; "Though appearing to . . ." chap. 17, v. 19; "It is not distant . . ." chap. 18, v. 5; "Having

finally recognized . . ." chap. 18, v. 8; "He who sees reality . . ." chap. 18, v. 15; His actions in this . . ." chap. 18, v. 13; "Not seeing, he . . ." chap. 18, v. 15.

131 *Ghost Dance: Prologue* and *Ghost Dance.* The Ghost Dance movement, a complicated series of interacting cults, apparently originated about 1869 among the Paviotso Indians near Walker Lake in Nevada. During the next thirty years, the religious movement spread in varying forms to the Washo, Klamath, Modoc, Shasta, Sioux and other tribes throughout nearly the entire western portion of the United States. Messianic in character, the Ghost Dance cults anticipated a time when the Indian dead would return, and when all white people would die or disappear. Such desperate and farfetched beliefs were probably stimulated and encouraged by the extreme deprivation and dislocation that many of the tribes were undergoing; the cults in turn were sometimes blamed for encouraging militancy among the Indians.

In terms of historical chronology, the section entitled *Ghost Dance: Prologue* should follow rather than precede *Ghost Dance* because it is based on events of the 1890 phase of the movement which spread chiefly east of the Rockies, while *Ghost Dance* refers to the 1870 phase of the movement, which flourished west of the Rockies. Although both phases originated among the Paviotso and sprang from a common cultural tradition, they were separate and distinct events, inspired by two different prophets.

131 *Ghost Dance: Prologue* is based on "Statement of American Horse, Delivered in council at Pine Ridge agency to Agent Royer, and forwarded to the Indian Office, November 27, 1890." Government Document 37002-1890. Quoted from James Mooney: *The Ghost-Dance Religion and the Sioux Outbreak of 1890,* edited by Anthony F. C. Wallace,

University of Chicago Press, 1965. (© 1965 by The University of Chicago) American Horse was a leader on the Sioux reservations in the Dakotas.

Merton's source for *Ghost Dance* is Cora DuBois, "The 1870 Ghost Dance," University of California Publications in Anthropological Records, Volume III (1939-1946), No. 1. Merton has used many phrases and direct quotations from the DuBois report, but he has also done a great deal of selection and condensation from her long and detailed account. "Doctor Sam," "Minnie Jo," "John Watchino," and "Annie Peterson" were DuBois' Indian informants. Wodziwob lived near Walker Lake in Nevada, about 1870. An adherent and assistant of his was apparently the father of Wovoka, also called Jack Wilson, who became known as "The Messiah," the most famous proponent of the later Ghost Dance cult of 1890. "Dr. Frank" was Frank Spencer, also widely known as Weneyuga. "Captain Jack," a leader of the Modocs, is also noted for leading his people in a fierce resistance to the whites. The quote from the *Cornwallis Gazette* (Stanza 23) is found in DuBois, page 26. "Coquille Charlie," actually named "Coquille Thompson," was one of DuBois' informants and had himself been a religious leader in his youth. His accounts of the Ghost Dance differ from those of Annie Peterson and other informants; he was apparently involved in one of the later and more corrupt manifestations of the cult. He should not be confused with earlier leaders such as "Depot Charlie" or "Klamath Charlie." The Warm House Dance, Dream Dance, and Feather Dance were later versions of the Ghost Dance ritual. DuBois points out that by the time of the Feather Dance, the religious significance was gone, and the "supernatural inspiration disregarded." (Dr. DuBois' material is used by permission of The Regents of the University of California.)